August 29, 2005

To: Clark & Melia Lee

Gwendolyn Fay Cummings

Grasshopper Pilot

Grasshopper Pilot

A MEMOIR

Julian William Cummings

with

Gwendolyn Kay Cummings

The Kent State University Press

KENT & LONDON

© 2005 by The Kent State University Press, Kent, Ohio 44242
ALL RIGHTS RESERVED

Library of Congress Catalog Card Number 2004029966
ISBN 0-87338-832-1
Manufactured in the United States of America

09   08   07   06   05   5   4   3   2   1

Library of Congress Cataloging-in-Publication Data

Cummings, Julian William, 1915–2002.
Grasshopper pilot : a memoir / Julian William Cummings
with Gwendolyn Kay Cummings.
p.   cm.
1. Cummings, Julian William, 1915–2002. 2. United States. Army.
Infantry Division, 3rd. 3. World War, 1939–1945—Aerial operations,
American. 4. World War, 1939–1945—Artillery operations, American.
5. World War, 1939–1945—Personal narratives, American. 6. Piper Cubs
(Airplanes) 7. Air pilots, Military—United States—Biography.
I. Cummings, Gwendolyn Kay, 1925– II. Title.
D769.33rd .C86 2005
940.54'4973'092—dc22   2004029966

British Library Cataloging-in-Publication data are available.

This book is dedicated to all the men in my aviation section
of the Third Infantry Division, U.S. Field Artillery

Contents

Acknowledgments

Special thanks to grasshopper pilots Lt. Col. Paynee O. Lysne, Capt. Alfred Schultz, Capt. Mike Strok (who was also editor of the *L-4 Grasshopper Wing* newsletter), and Maj. Frances A. Even, engineer, each of whom provided valuable information or photos to substantiate and augment the events described in this book.

We also thank our good friends Lillian Dearinger and Jim Hansen for their patient advice and assistance with early versions of the manuscript and our family, who encouraged and supported us in getting this book completed.

Many thanks to Lowell McClellan, who skillfully prepared the final manuscript for submission to the publisher.

Introduction

Many articles and books have been written, and movies made, about the battles of every branch of the military. However, there is one group of men that has been forgotten, ignored, or is just plain unknown to most people. I refer to those affectionately called the "Grasshopper pilots," the men who flew dangerous missions in unarmed Piper Cubs during World War II.

The purpose of this book is to tell the story of these heroic pilots, who fearlessly performed their duties as air observers for the field artillery; as angels of mercy, evacuating the wounded or delivering vital medical supplies; and as doers of countless other impossible missions. These daring men were constantly in the thick of battle. They were the eyes of the field artillery. Their primary purpose was observation, a continual mission of locating enemy gun locations and radioing their positions back to the command post. By doing this they actually directed the artillery shells to the target. The only defense against an assault on the Piper Cubs was the pilots' ability to outmaneuver enemy fighter planes and dodge gunfire, sometimes "friendly."

All the experiences in this book are true. They are but a few of the countless events in the lives of the Grasshopper pilots. In the following chapters you will learn of some of my own missions and the experiences of others close to me.

JULIAN WILLIAM CUMMINGS

· 1 ·

Born to Fly

I was born on December 17, 1915. That was the twelfth anniversary of the first heavier-than-air flight made by man at Kitty Hawk, North Carolina. I was born to fly. Now, that sounds a little egotistical; nevertheless, flying influenced my life in my early years, and in later years it put wings on me.

The very first thing I remember as far as flying was concerned happened one day when I was four, maybe five, years old. We were living in Salt Lake City on the south slope of the north hills. Aviation was still in its infancy, and to see an airplane was quite a novelty. It was a cloudy day. Suddenly there was a roar outside, and everybody in the family ran out on the front porch to see what it was. An airplane was flying over the top of the house, and we thought it was going to knock the bricks off the chimney. It didn't—it headed west to the airport about fourteen miles away. To the best of my recollection, that was my first experience with flying.

The years rolled by, and when I was about eleven years old Lindbergh crossed the Atlantic Ocean and in the process became America's hero. He visited city after city, and Salt Lake City hosted him, in its turn, one memorable morning. We young boys who belonged to the Mormon Church's Boy Trail Builders (similar to the Cub Scouts) were all down at Liberty Park to view Lindbergh as he came around the oval street in the center of the park.

We were standing there waiting when somebody shouted, "There he is, high in the sky!" In the southeast was a silver monoplane, and it headed north-west toward the Salt Lake Airport. Everyone was screaming, "There he is! There he is! There's Lucky—Lucky Lindy flying high up in the sky!" We waited and waited. Soon a big open touring car came around the bend of Liberty Park. In

1

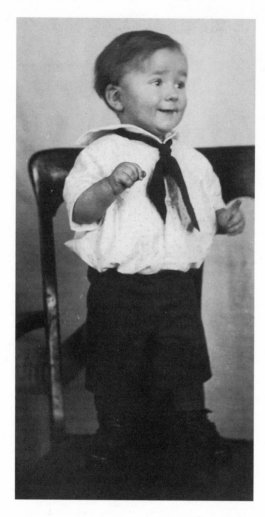

*Enthusiastic Billy
Cummings, even
at age one.*

it was Lindy, sitting high on the back with all the dignitaries—the mayor, the governor, and who knows who else. All eyes were on Lindy, the man who had flown alone across the Atlantic Ocean. I didn't fully understand the implication of this great feat, but to me it was wonderful. My heart pounded in my chest at seeing this remarkable pilot who had become such a hero.

Time went by, and my uncle, Dean R. Brimhall, was opening the Ogden, Utah, airport, which he owned. He had brought in an autogiro for the celebration. My dad took me to the airport. Oh, what a thrill to see an autogiro, which was the closest thing there was to a helicopter in those days. Dad was going to go for a ride, and Uncle Dean said to him, "Julian, I want you to take a ride."

I begged, "Can I go? Can I go?"

My dad said, "Little boys are to be seen and not heard." I didn't go for a ride that day, but my dad did. When I got home I found a two-by-four about twelve inches long and cut a couple of one-by-fours out of scrap lumber for wings. I put them on the two-by-four like a biplane and made an improvised plane. I tried to get something I could use for wheels, made a spinner prop, and that was my first airplane. It was a crude one, but it was mine, and I loved it.

Max Bodine was a good friend of mine, and his dad was chief mechanic at Western Air Express. We would ride our bikes down there and just wish we could go for an airplane ride. Neither of us got a ride on those airplanes. I remember once seeing a Boeing, which could fly four people under the hood as passengers. We would watch them take off and others come in. Later on Tommy Thompson, who was my local hero, had a twin-engine plane, but I *still* didn't get a ride. I never *did* get a ride.

Sometime later I found some articles in one of the magazines (*Popular Science* or *Popular Mechanics*) titled "Barn Storm," by Randy Enslow, who used to barnstorm with Lindbergh. He was going to teach us to fly in those articles. So I would sit in one of my mother's kitchen chairs and get the broomstick out. That was the joystick. I would put my feet out like I had pedals behind them.

Now you're ready for takeoff. Push the throttle ahead, neutralize the stick, now pull back a little on the stick. You have some speed coming up. Go ahead and gradually push the stick ahead a little bit to neutralize the altitude, and pick up some more speed. Now, let's make a left turn. Push in on the left rudder and also push the stick to the left. Don't push the stick down too far or you might dive. If you pull it back too far, you might stall out. All right, neutralize your stick, and neutralize your rudder pedals. Now you're heading in the other direction. Now let's make a right turn. Push on the right rudder pedals. Push the stick to the right. Neutralize the stick. Neutralize your pedal. Now you've made a right turn.

He had us make climbs and gain altitude. He told us how to watch our instruments. I learned how to fly in my mother's kitchen. Flying around with Enslow in the kitchen left much to be desired, but at least the desire to learn to fly was still in my bosom, even though I hadn't been off the ground yet.

My one cousin, Rulon Cummings, and I went up to Roy, Utah, to visit another cousin of ours, Arnold Hardy. We went down to talk to the kid who lived just south of Arnold. We started talking, and I suggested that we build an airplane. Rulon said, "What are you talking about?" I told him that we could build a glider. I told them to get some one-by-two lumber and that we could use some of the canvas off his dad's chicken coop. We made a wing about six feet long and two feet wide and a couple of longerons that I could grab hold of with my hands. We put a tail on the longerons about two feet to the rear. We got it all set up. There was a tail surface, and there was a wing surface. I got up in the barn, and they handed the contraption up to me. The tail just fit inside the entrance to the hayloft.

I looked at the pile of straw about twenty feet out ahead and said, "I'm going to make it to that pile of straw." They looked up at me and kind of shook their heads. I yelled, "Okay, here I go!" and I jumped. Well, I hit a pile all right, but it wasn't a pile of straw—it was a pile of manure directly below me. You see, what I failed to take into consideration was wing loading. I knew nothing about wing loading. I wasn't an aeronautical engineer; I was just a kid building an airplane. Anyway, the aircraft, such as it was, broke my fall.

In 1934, when I was nineteen years old, the Mormon Church called me on a mission to Argentina. I had a companion who loved airplanes. He had worked at the airport in Central Deglaja in Central America but had never learned to fly. We both loved flying and would go out to the airport at Secareo and look up at the planes, wishing we could fly.

I completed my mission in 1936 and returned home to Utah, where I started working at Utah Copper and enrolled in classes at the University of Utah in Salt Lake City. In 1938 I married my sweetheart, Marjorie Kane. Working fulltime, going to college, and fulfilling my responsibilities at home and at church often allowed me less than four hours' sleep at night. I felt lucky to have a job, but our budget was tight with few luxuries. In spite of my heavy financial obligations, I was determined to fly even if I had to pay for lessons. I stopped off at the field at South Salt Lake Airport and took a lesson from Vern Carter in a Piper Cub. Vern had been with Uncle Dean at Ogden Airport. By this time, Uncle Dean had gone to Washington, D.C., to help set up the Civil Aeronautics Administration, so Vern opened his own school down in South Salt Lake. Vern had written the course for the government program. It was Pilot Course 2 of the Civil Aeronautics Administration. What a fantastic thing the government had done. It saw the handwriting on the wall, with a war coming on and few trained to fly. There were some exceptions, a few select people who had gone to Kelly Field and into the Navy to learn to fly. There were also some who had paid good prices at civilian pilot training schools.

At this time I applied to get into Navy flying, and the flight sergeant told me that everything was "go." I had the education, and I was in top shape physically, but he told me that the Navy was only taking 500 pilot trainees a year and that the quota was filled for that year. Again, my heart sank, but I was determined. My plan at this time was to get into Navy flight training and then go into the Marines as a fighter pilot, as a number of my friends had done. This did not work, so in early 1940 I decided to take Pilot Course 2 at the University of Utah. Upon completion of the course I received my wings from the university.

To build up more hours of flying experience, I bought into a club. There were twenty-seven members in the club, and only six of us knew how to fly. It was nice of those other twenty-one guys to help us pay for our new airplane, a brand-new Taylor Craft.

One morning in the summer of 1941, I went down to get my flight physical. When I went into Dr. Vance's office, I didn't feel very good. He told me to lie down on the table and said he would be back in a few minutes. Forty-five minutes later he came back, and I immediately got up. I felt a little dizzy, and when he wrapped my arm to take my blood pressure, I passed out. A few weeks later there was a knock at my door. When I opened the door, there stood Mr. Hughes from the Civil Aeronautics Administration.

He said, "I have come here for your license."

"What do you want with my license?" I asked.

He said, "You passed out in Dr. Vance's office. You can no longer fly. The orders are from Washington, and if you want to know more about it you will have to write to them."

I had to give him my license. However, I still kept flying my club's plane until I sold out to Meg Jensen, who was a secretary out at Utah Copper. She bought my membership when I was called to active duty.

When I graduated from the Reserve Officers Training Corps unit at the University of Utah, I received my second lieutenant's commission in the Field Artillery and was sent to Camp Roberts, California. Once I got there I still wanted to fly, so I decided to look into going through cadet training as an officer. I was getting ready to fill out my papers when the artillery said that all the officers who had sixty hours or more of private flying were to put in for flight training at Fort Sill, Oklahoma, for specialized training. I immediately applied. I was chosen to be one of the first combat pilots in the invasion of Africa.

· 2 ·

How the Grasshopper Came to Be

The adoption and formation of observation planes for the Army did not happen overnight. Numerous trials and maneuvers were performed before the Army could reach a decision. It knew what it wanted observation planes to do, but it was unable at first to find the kind of aircraft that would perform properly.

It was in the early 1940s, and the military was holding some of these maneuvers in Texas. A lot of the upper brass thought it might be a good idea to have observation planes for the Army. The Army Air Corps came out with the O-46 and O-47. These were large planes. One of them weighed about two tons. These airplanes needed a long runway. That wasn't at all what we wanted. We wanted something organic, something that would allow close contact with our artillery units. We needed to get up and take off in a small space, and we needed to be close to the front lines. We had to have a plane we could fly to locate enemy gun positions or movement and radio the information to the artillery. While we were up there, we needed to adjust the artillery fire. We needed *that* kind of airplane, and these monsters were not right for us.

Some of the authorities decided to let the civilian aircraft people (Piper, Aeronca, and Taylor Craft) send some of their own boys down, at their own expense, to fly their types of aircraft. Old Hank Wann from Piper Aircraft flew in over the desert using a short-field procedure, landing over a barrier, taking off over a barrier, and hopping around. As Wann got out of his Piper Cub and walked in, the commanding general of the Second Cavalry Division said, "You look like a bunch of damn grasshoppers out there." The name took and became the symbol for military light planes.

Lt. Julian William (Bill) Cummings, commissioned Grasshopper pilot.

During maneuvers at Camp Polk, Louisiana, Col. Dwight D. Eisenhower, who himself was a licensed pilot, became an enthusiastic supporter of the Grasshoppers. The final verdict on the Grasshoppers' performance during the summer and fall Army maneuvers was that they were indispensable. They could take off and land on the same roads used by armored units, and they could use the same gasoline, rather than high-octane fuel. The Grasshoppers didn't need a hard surface runway, and their maintenance and repair requirements were simple.

In June 1942 the War Department approved the formation of a special branch of the Army officially dubbed Organic Air Observation for the Field Artillery, meaning they were now considered an integral part of the organization. Thus, the Grasshoppers became not only official but also finally and formally recognized as a vital part of military strategy. We had a song that we often sang to the tune of "Field Artillery" ("Over Here, Over There . . ."). It said something about our being as hard to find as fleas and that "we'll give the

Axis fits" with our "Maytag Messerschmitts" but also repeated a refrain that said that we were the "eyes of the field artillery."

As official as the Grasshoppers had become, there still were scores of civilians and military who didn't have any idea that the Grasshopper existed. Most people in the service didn't know what a Grasshopper pilot was. At first they were unaware that these Piper Cubs and their pilots were making a big difference in the war effort.

In the invasion of Sicily one of those Cubs, in a two-and-a-half-hour flight, saved 15,000 lives, according to Gen. George S. Patton Jr. How many fighters and how many bombers have made that short a mission and saved that many lives? The only one I can think of is the *Enola Gay*, which helped stop the invasion of Japan and kept us from losing thousands of our boys going in there. That's the only plane I can think of other than this little Piper Cub.

The Grasshoppers were used for many risky tasks. Besides observation and artillery fire control, they were the eyes in the sky for detecting troop movements, communication centers, and supply installations. They ran aerial resupply, aerial evacuation of the sick and wounded, and aerial photography and message relay. They located motor convoys and did camouflage inspection. They were rapid transportation for senior officers as well as unit commanders.

An article by Konrad F. Schreier in *Aviation History*, "How the Grasshopper Earned Its Wings" (May 1996), observed that "the Army did not even call them airplanes, classing them officially as 'vehicles.' Nevertheless, they directed much of the deadly U.S. Army field artillery fire, the most effective in the conflict" (34).

The Grasshopper pilots were referred to as the "hop, skip, and jump" pilots. Our unit was composed of tiny little Piper Cub planes, the kind people putt-putted around in before the war. But the work we did on the battlefield would curl the teeth of the toughest stunt flier.

"Grasshoppers," "Kites," "Cubs," "L-4s," "Maytag Messerschmitts," or whatever you want to call them, these babies got the job done better than anything else available for air observation during World War II.

·3·

Training at Fort Sill

It all dates back to when the field artillery had an urgent need for observation for directing the fire of guns and howitzers, when ground observation was inadequate. The cry went out for men in the ground forces who knew how to fly. I had flown some sixty-odd hours in the plane I had a part-interest in back in Salt Lake City. It was fun flying that little, light, high-wing monoplane out over the mountains.

I wanted to continue flying out over God's green earth and seeing it in all its splendor, both at home and overseas. How would it be to fly over the desert sands of North Africa, the green hills and dales of Europe, and the snow-capped peaks of the Alps? What would it be like to see the desert camel caravans, the wandering Bedouin tribes, and the white mosque–tipped villages silhouetting the desert fringe in the distance at eventide? How would it be to see the hardy Italian farmers tilling their soil from daylight to dark, wondering what the war was all about, wondering why their young men were being taken for the army just when they could do the most good on their meager plots of ground? What a thrill it would be to see the sapphire-blue Mediterranean Sea fringed by the rugged African coastline and the green-topped cliffs of Italy. Maybe I would even fly over the romantic Isle of Capri.

I entered the U.S. Army in June 1942. I had been enlisted for a mere six weeks and was just getting my teeth into running fresh recruits through basic training at Camp Roberts when I received those blessed orders: "Report to the Field Artillery School at Fort Sill, Oklahoma, Pilot Course 2 in Artillery Pilot Observation Training." I knew that as a field artillery officer I would sooner or later end up taking a course at Fort Sill, but I had never dreamed it would be a pilot's course.

I arrived there the middle of August 1942, as much an eager beaver as any of the other fifteen officers enrolled with me. The course was all new to us; in fact, it was new to everybody. I suppose a great many people have in the past believed us to be frauds, and some still think that. Wings usually go with the Air Force, and it is difficult for people to understand how an artilleryman can be a pilot in the Army.

For the next five weeks we learned how to break most of the civil air regulations that in the past civilian days we had obeyed religiously, in fear of being grounded. Keep 500 feet above the ground? Nonsense. Now we were being taught to fly *five* feet above the ground, in and out through the trees, down ravines, over tree lines, and down on the other side. We were tough now.

When the instructor yelled, "Zero," or "Messerschmitt," we would get down to Mother Earth in the quickest possible manner, land in the nearest cow pasture or the most convenient road, and tail the plane in under the trees before the simulated enemy plane could get at us.

We learned how to take off in the shortest possible space, over barriers at the end of the landing strip. We had short-field landings and takeoffs, contour flying, and evasive maneuvers pounded into us as much as it could be in the short time allotted. At the same time, we were taught how to maintain our little "Maytag Messerschmitts" in the field, with the minimum of equipment and under rugged conditions.

Many times during training I cursed under my breath at our flight instructor, Mr. Reeves, for yelling at me time after time, "Watch your altitude," or "Hold that nose down on your turns." Later, I silently and prayerfully thanked him. He taught me to make the many maneuvers automatically in the safest way possible. You can't stop to think about how to do a certain maneuver when Jerry is on your tail or when enemy ground fire is coming up at you thick and fast. You just do the same type of flying you have been right along. If you were cocky and didn't listen to your instructor in the early days and didn't form good flying habits, you could easily and unwittingly stall out of a turn too close to the ground and burn in the wreckage. This happened to one of my buddies in the early part of the Tunisian campaign.

The last week of our training took us out into the field to teach us what we were to do for the field artillery in action. Our instructor, a Captain Hauser, brought us to a field of tall grass surrounded by large trees that offered top cover. "Here," he said, "you will prepare a landing strip, set up communications, and camouflage your planes after dispersing them."

The weeds were about three feet high. Landing on this field, one would certainly nose over and break a prop, or even worse. We had to figure some way to make it useable. If we were out in combat and had only a small truck, like we did now, the only choice would be to find a large log or old harrow and tie it behind the truck, drag the strip, knock the weeds down, and clear the rocks and rubble away from it. This we did, much to the satisfaction of the instructor. We soon set up our communications and dispersed and camouflaged our planes. We were then ready to test our ability in knocking out the enemy.

"Fly about 500 feet above the ground and stay to the rear and off to one side of your guns. You are only to be used when no other means of observation is available. You must remember that your planes are very vulnerable and won't last too long if used very often and too close to the front lines," said Captain Hauser.

I can say that even though the words seemed very reasonable at the time combat had not yet proven what could be done with our versatile little Grasshopper planes. Up we went, 500 feet above the ground and to the rear of the guns.

"Enemy machine guns. Base point is 500 left, 200. Over," I called over the radio, giving an offset to the target from a known reference point using the map grid.

"On the way" (meaning the guns had fired) came back the answer after a short pause. Pretty close, but not close enough.

"Five zero right, repeat range, fire for effect," I again called in.

"Battery firing for effect," they responded.

Right on the nose. Now, if they had only been real German machine guns, I would have liked it much better. Already I was eager to get a shot at them.

We finished the course on September 12, 1942, and felt like we knew all about knocking out the enemy—"Just let us at them and we'll show them!" They did let us at them, and sooner than we expected.

· 4 ·

Invasion of North Africa

We had just finished a short five-day leave (it took me two days to reach home and two days to return) after our flight training at Fort Sill when we received orders to move out to various units. My orders said to report to the Third Artillery Division at Camp Pickett, Virginia. Good. A lot of my buddies from the University of Utah were in that outfit. Joining them would be like Old Home Week.

En route to base one evening, I was sitting in a restaurant and noticed an Army Air Corps officer staring at me. As I got up to go, he motioned for me to come over to his table. "What's the idea of wearing wings with field artillery crossed-cannon insignia?" he demanded quite abruptly.

"Have you ever heard of the Grasshopper pilots?" I queried.

"No," he answered.

"Well, someday, lieutenant, you will probably hear a lot about us," I responded. It was just before the invasion of Africa.

It was far from Old Home Week at the base for any of us. Four of our group had only half an hour to get ready and head for the aircraft carrier USS *Ranger*, based at a different port than New York, where the rest of us were going, where they would find planes ready for them.

Our short stay at Camp Pickett was a waiting game. Our excitement ran at a fever pitch; we knew that we were headed for an invasion but not sure where. Many of the men spent these hours engaged in nervous banter or playing cards. For others it was a chance for sober reflection. When things were quiet I would try to imagine what it would be like, flying my new plane. I knew it

12

was somewhere in the hold of our waiting ship, unassembled and packed in a crate just as it was when it left the Piper Cub factory. I felt some comfort knowing that my Cub and I would arrive at our destination at the same time. I knew also that my first assignment on arrival at our destination would be to assemble it with whatever resources available, under whatever conditions existed, and make it flyable. I marveled at the strange calm I felt, even though my little plane was totally unusable at that moment.

We knew this was going to be the start of the big push to rid the world of Hitler's and Mussolini's terror. We knew that everything we would encounter in the coming months would be foreign to us. We were all trained for our military assignments, but being trained and actually facing the horrors of war are two entirely different matters. Who among that mass of brave troops would survive? No one knew for sure, but I know each of us was hoping that we would be among the lucky.

The possibility of being killed in action certainly haunted everyone's dreams. In my own case, I had been promised through a special blessing given by one of our church leaders that I would not have a drop of my blood spilled in battle. My assignment was an especially risky one, and I should have had serious thoughts about death, yet I felt at peace because of the promise.

Still, the probability of being killed was not as great as some feared. I remember that Gen. George S. Patton had once said in a prebattle pep talk that only 2 percent of the troops would die in a major battle. Even if his calculation was accurate, it was little comfort for many of our troops at a time like this.

Patton also said that every soldier in the Army played a vital part in the war effort, that every job is an essential part of the whole scheme of things. So he knew the critical role the Grasshoppers would play in the upcoming invasion. He knew the Grasshoppers wouldn't let him down and that their efforts would save thousands of our men's lives and help bring this ugly war to an end.

There was good reason for Patton's confidence in our ability to assist the battle plan. He had been an early proponent of lightweight aerial observation craft after having seen them perform successfully during World War I. The fact that he was a licensed pilot and owned a small plane himself only heightened his zeal to get them approved by the military. As he rose through the ranks during the 1920s, he made repeated efforts to get the Army to utilize them, and by the time World War II broke out Patton was using lightweight reconnaissance aircraft in all his military maneuvers. So it was no last-minute decision on his part to include us in his tactics as he led the invasion of North

Generals Patton, Bradley, and Eisenhower observe lightweight plane maneuvers. Notice the Stinson L-5 in the background. Courtesy Bill Stratton, international liaison pilot, Aircraft Association.

Africa. Patton never missed an occasion to express pride in his role as a pioneer of the Grasshoppers, and he often reminded his troops of the vital contribution we were making to the success of the war effort.

Patton's speeches prepared most of us for what we knew was just around the corner by shaping our attitudes for the conflict in which we were about to engage. With this mindset, we were ready for the voyage that would bring us face to face with our enemies.

The invasion of North Africa had been set for early dawn on November 8, 1942, though we were not told of the exact time and place. The Allied fleets were to sail out of British ports at the same time that our convoy, loaded with men and munitions, was to leave from New York's harbor. The American troops would cross 3,100 miles of the Atlantic and rendezvous with our allies somewhere off the coast of North Africa. The *Ranger* would meet up with our ships soon after.

The magnitude of this convoy was awesome beyond imagination. Some 65,000 soldiers from the United States, joined by 61,000 Allied troops, sailed at the same time and headed for Africa. We weren't alone; joining us were 700 ships carrying 22 million pounds of food, 36 million pounds of clothing, 10 million gallons of gasoline, and more than a million copies of 10,100 different maps. In addition, there were hundreds of tanks and bulldozers, tons of ammunition, and big guns by the thousands.

This invasion was called Operation Torch. Never before in history had so large a mechanized army ever attempted to land on a hostile shore. When the Allies landed it was the first time our troops met the Nazis on the battlefield. We knew this was the beginning of the march to Berlin. This convoy was magnificent.

We loaded ourselves onto the ship heading for the invasion. Now, I think we all knew what we were going to be doing, but we had not yet received our orders. Nevertheless, in the truck going down to the dock everyone was singing a tune, "Little French Ditties." We were going to French Morocco, North Africa.

Once we got aboard, we busied ourselves finding the right bunk and getting acquainted with the group. Finally, things settled down, and the poker games started. I'm not much of a poker player, and the one that I sat in on was for a ten-cent limit. Just for fun we kicked a few dimes around on the top of the table.

The men were all talking about the various cities along the coastline that we would encounter, the main one being Casablanca. As night came on, everybody became a little weary and edgy. Some of the men said, "Hey, look out there!" Their imaginations had run away with them, and they thought U-boats might come and lower the boom on us in that big task force. But it never happened.

The rumbles, squeaks, and groans of all of the vessels as they surged through the rough ocean waters created an uneasy, eerie atmosphere. Just knowing the odds against all of us returning to our homeland and families again was terrifying. It was the longest night of my life. I thought of my home and my family.

My wife, Maggie—how I longed for her. Mom and Dad, with their gentle, caring manner, were concerned for their four sons in different parts of the world serving their country—what a burden they carried. I wondered if life would ever return to any kind of normalcy. Closing my day with a prayer, as I'm sure many of the others in this convey did, I finally drifted into a troubled sleep.

Early on the morning of November 8, the aircraft carrier *Ranger* joined our convoy. Of all the pilots aboard the carrier, there were only three who had aircraft that were assembled: Captain Devol and Captain Alcorn each took one, and Lieutenant Butler and Lieutenant Shell took the third to fly ashore. There they were, sixty miles out from the African coastline, too far away to see it.

"You mean we're heading into land from here, and we can't even see the blasted shore?" questioned Lieutenant Butler.

"That's right," answered Captain Devol. "They're supposed to set up a field for us at a predetermined spot at Fedala, just north of Casablanca. Our troops are landing there, and with luck we'll make it about the time they have the place cleared of the enemy."

They got their maps ready and warmed up their planes. It would be the first aircraft carrier takeoff any of the Grasshoppers had made, but they were ready for it. Short-field work at Fort Sill had taught them how to take off from much shorter fields than the carrier's flight deck. Shortly after all three took off, one of the planes lurched, and a terrific explosion pierced the air.

"What the hell was that?" yelled Butler across to Devol.

"Take a look off to your right and see for yourself, man!" answered Devol. "The whole blasted Navy is trying their damnedest to shoot us down! I'm heading for just above the crests of the waves." From then on they "contoured" the waves all the way in to the shore.

Nervous and inexperienced Navy gunners had not received sufficient training in aircraft recognition. How were they to know the Army or Navy had a mess of Piper Cubs flying all over the invasion front? It wasn't just the Navy that was trigger-happy when the Cubs came flying over; some infantrymen who had only a few moments earlier been strafed by a Heinkel bomber took a few pot shots at the low-flying Cub on the horizon just ahead of them. As Captain Alcorn came in from the south, all they could see was the prop and the wings, and they couldn't see any markings. Rounds of .50-caliber bullets bombarded his helpless Cub, and down came Captain Alcorn in flames. He crash-landed in a field near the shore, where he spent some harrowing hours in unfriendly territory. Some time later he was rescued and evacuated to a

U.S. hospital ship with two slugs in his leg. Fortunately, it didn't kill him; but later, when I inspected the crash site, I counted eighteen holes in his engine. He was lucky to get out of the burning plane. He was sent back to the States.

That was the first casualty of our Grasshopper pilots, and also the first medal awarded; he got the Purple Heart. Lieutenants Shell and Butler were also forced down by enemy fire. They landed in the vicinity of a French fort, where they were captured; they remained prisoners of the French for some time. Captain Devol made it in one hop. He became the first U.S. pilot to land on French African soil.

The rest of us walked down the gangplank. The crates that housed our aircraft were loaded into trucks and transported to the Casablanca airport. We had fun getting our little Piper Cubs ready to go. We went down to the airport to put them together. We couldn't find enough tools, so I headed to Casablanca. First I asked the Air Corps for tools, and they told me to get them from the Army. "You're Army," they said. I went to the Army, and they told me to go to the Air Corps. "You're flying airplanes," they said. Army Field Artillery Air Observation was so new that they hadn't even assigned us to an organizational chart yet. Back and forth we went, so I headed into Casablanca to the black market and bought a bunch of tools. Most of them were metric, but they came in handy later. After some time, we finally got our planes assembled and ready for action.

All of the pilots had taken off except Captain Devol and myself. I propped his plane (spun the propeller by hand to start the engine) and got his engine going, ready for takeoff. He was waiting for me to go.

I got out behind my prop. We had been taught how to prop our aircraft from the rear so we could immediately get into the cockpit, slap the throttle cord, and take off. These stiff engines were brand new, however, and just didn't kick in that fast. I got out in front, but I made the mistake of not putting chocks in front of the wheels. I pulled that baby through, and she started taking off. I had cracked the throttle a little too much. I moved so the prop wouldn't hit me, but the wing strut got me in the belly. I got in the plane and pushed the throttle closed, and looked over at Devol. He was laughing.

I said, "I know what I'm going to call this critter: *Maggie the Runaway*— 'Maggie' after my wife, and 'runaway' after my first incident with my airplane." We then took off to meet at our rendezvous point. I wrote to my wife that night and told her what had happened, and she said I should call my plane *Maggie the Faithful*. And that's what I called my Cub from then on.

Bill with Maggie the Faithful *at Rabat, ready to take off for Oujda to sign in.*

We went up to Rabat and joined our unit there. Shortly after we got things moved around, I received orders to go up to Guercief, to the Thirtieth Infantry. From there I was to fly border patrol along the Spanish-Moroccan border. Lt. Jim Bailey would be with me.

Arriving at Guercief, I reported to Col. "Buck" Rogers for duty. Upon reading my orders, he told me that the orders had been written in such a way that I had to sign in at the battalion headquarters at Oujda, quite a distance to the east of where we were. He told me he had a 250-pound captain with bedroll

Bill preparing to patrol French Moroccan border before the invasion of Sicily.

and luggage for me to fly as a passenger to Oujda. I thought that was a lot of weight for my little Army Piper L-4. I reminded him that it was getting late, but he informed me that we had plenty of time before nightfall and that we could make it. My concern was that I had no night-flying training.

All gassed up and fully loaded, we took off with only a Socony Vacuum road map for navigation. About two-thirds of the way there, the sun was setting fast, so I flew down and hugged the road. There were no hills in the area, just a straight, level road. There was a partial moon, and it was a clear night.

I flew over the area that should have been the airport, but it wasn't there. I very nervously flew on. Finally I spotted Oujda, its buildings silhouetted on the horizon. I looked again at my road map with my GI flashlight, and it showed the airport to be located at the southeast side of the town, but I could see no runways, no aircraft anywhere.

Gas tanks don't get filled flying around looking for an airport, so I picked what appeared to be a flat field just outside of town and gave it a low drag, came around again, and set *Maggie the Faithful* down for a bumpy landing. I cut the throttle and got out to look around. I had landed in a field of boulders as big as my head. My horizontal stabilizer had been torn hitting one of those rocks.

Moroccans began to gather around, filled with curiosity. Since neither the captain nor I spoke Arabic, communication with these people was highly improbable. I was concerned. Were they friend or foe? Were we out of harm's way? Not knowing what might happen, we decided to sleep in my cramped cockpit until daylight. I tried to settle my six-foot frame down as best I could in the tiny space available. As uncomfortable as I was, I wondered how my oversized passenger could find any comfort in the undersized backseat of my Cub. But even in his cramped position he had somehow drifted off into slumber. Morning couldn't come too soon, I thought. Despite the captain's nerve-wracking snores, fatigue took control of my body and removed me from the troubled circumstances surrounding me.

At daybreak I was abruptly awakened by a thump on the cockpit door. There, peering in through the window, was a GI from the battalion headquarters in Oujda. "Are you guys having some trouble here?"

"What in the world happened to the airport that was supposed to be here?" I asked. "It shows one on my map, but it's not here."

"Oh, that must be an old map you have. The airport's in the opposite direction, twelve miles north of here. I'm here to help you repair your plane and then take the captain to headquarters while you fly your plane to the airport near the base."

We repaired the stabilizer as best we could with the tools from my toolbox. As soon as I became airborne the captain and the GI jumped in his jeep and headed back to headquarters. After reporting in at the battalion headquarters in Oujda, I flew back to Guercief.

At first I thought this desert life would be drab work, but now and then a bright spot would shine through. One time, on the colonel's birthday, we found that we only had one turkey; we needed more meat for this occasion. I volunteered to go out with an observer, fly over a herd of gazelles (African antelope), and get one with a Tommy gun. I located a herd, and as I flew down closer to them, my observer shot into the herd. One of the gazelles fell, so we landed the plane and picked it up. This little trick brought the meat home for the colonel's birthday dinner. And on several occasions we had to land at small villages in the desert. Every time we landed the whole town would turn out, and the mayor would invite us to his home. Often we were invited on boar hunts and mountain goat hunts by these mayors. On several occasions we were invited to banquets by the chiefs.

After about five months of desert experiences, I was ordered to join my artillery unit and head for Tunisia. As I flew east I ran into some weather problems. The pass ahead was socked in so bad that I didn't feel it was advisable to penetrate it with my Piper Cub without radio communication. I had been following a railroad track for visual navigation. I saw a French colonial town

No place to land except the railroad tracks.

at the entrance of the pass and looked around for a place to set my Cub down to wait out the cloud bank ahead. This cloud bank seemed to guard the pass and say "no entrance" to any little plane flying its way. The river was to the left of the track, with rolling hills beyond its left bank; the town was to the right.

I circled back and came in low over the tracks. The railroad bed seemed smooth enough, so I throttled back and set *Maggie the Faithful* down easy over the narrow-gauge tracks. As I came to a rattling stop, I saw a group of people running in my direction, a French colonel followed by some troops, mixed with French civilians.

I emerged from the cramped cockpit just as the colonel approached. We saluted. He welcomed me in broken English and asked if they could help in any way. Between my garbled French and his fragmented English, he understood my need to remain grounded until Mother Nature gave me clear skies and a cheery takeoff.

As the colonel arranged for his men to move my plane off to the side of the track and tie it down, he offered me a place to stay in their bivouac area. However, a French family that was in the group ran down to greet me, shouting *"Vive l'Amérique"* and offering—almost insisting—that I partake of their hospitality. Inasmuch as I had acquired some conversational French and had a yen to try French family-style cooking, I asked the colonel what he thought. He seemed quite agreeable to the invitation and said he would keep in touch with me and then ordered a couple of his troops to pitch their tent and guard my plane until I was able to take off again.

All went well at this fine family home at first. They were middle-class and had a comfortable home with plenty of room. However, after a couple of days, they seemed to grow uneasy, and I couldn't blame them. I asked the mother to tell me what the matter was. She said that when I landed they had noticed by my wedding ring that I was married. They would be overjoyed to have an American officer who was helping to free their people stay overnight. But, she said, even to the broad-minded French, the several-day stay that the cloudy weather had imposed was beginning to be embarrassing. You see, the father had been interned in France by the Germans, and that left Mama and three beautiful teenage daughters to take care of the home front until Papa could eventually return.

Mother Nature finally gave leave to the clouds that night, so the next morning I was on my way again. It seemed that half the town was out to watch the takeoff. As I started to throttle forward, I noticed off to the right Mama and her lovely teenage daughters, with tears in their eyes, waving me a fond farewell. They were wonderful people, good teachers, and their hospitality was greatly appreciated. Many times in months to come, I was grateful for the lessons in French grammar they had given me in exchange for the English lessons I had given them.

Just prior to our arrival in Tunisia, where my good friend Lt. Gordon Barney was, the Germans had come down on our forces with a vengeance. Our men were ordered to retreat. The pilots were ordered to destroy their airplanes and leave with the other troops.

Barney said, "Bull! I want to save my airplane!" He and another pilot took off in a cloud of dust in their Piper Cubs, just as German tanks advanced onto the field. Down the strip they went, slowly lifting from the ground. By the time the Cubs were airborne, the tanks were so close that the planes passed just four feet above them. The other pilot was shot down; his plane burst into flames and plunged into the ground. If through some miracle he survived, he would have been taken prisoner of war; but we never heard from him again.

Miraculously, Barney escaped without any wounds. His airplane received a broken windshield. For his bravery, and for saving equipment that was badly needed, even though he had disobeyed the order to destroy his airplane and retreat with the other troops, Lieutenant Barney was awarded the Silver Star. He was the first Grasshopper pilot to be awarded this medal.

The battle of Kasserine Pass in western Tunisia put the American forces to the test. The Germans had been retreating and offering little resistance but decided to make a stand at the pass. Erwin Rommel's counterattack was the first real battle of Gen. Dwight D. Eisenhower's career. Ike's troops were caught off-guard and badly defeated in the first few days of fighting. The Allied forces held, however, and reinforcements rolled out of the west to strengthen their position. No Cubs had been assigned to help the artillery locate the hidden gun emplacements of the Germans, and our men were being unmercifully mowed down and pushed back.

Lieutenant Barney, who had just saved his Cub in the retreat from the Germans in northern Tunisia, came to the rescue. He flew over the battle area, located the enemy, and reported their positions. The powerful guns of the field artillery, including a new weapon they had just received, the bazooka, were employed in defeating the enemy at this point.

With Army Air Observation overhead, everything was visible. Lieutenant Barney and his observer used every tactic they knew to locate the enemy gun nests, helping turn the battle from retreat and defeat to victory and glory. Lieutenant Barney saved many lives in that battle. Rommel and his army were stopped.

Kasserine Pass made it clear to those in command that we needed more trained pilots, observers, and L-4s for Army observation. On February 3, 1943, Headquarters Fifth Army issued orders to nine officers and seven enlisted men in various units throughout North Africa, placing them on detached service to the Fifth Army Air Operations School at Sidi-Bel-Abbès, Algeria, which was then the home of the French Foreign Legion.

My good friend Lt. Col. Paynee O. Lysne, who was a lieutenant at the time and already a license pilot, was one of the officer students enrolled to become a Grasshopper pilot. Lysne later wrote in an article,[1]

After reporting to the school I was told along with two others by a tough-looking sergeant, "Do you see that large box? Well, in that box is an airplane, which you'll take out carefully, assemble it by the book, and tomorrow, you'll fly it. And that box will be your home for as long as you're here in the school." This school was a one-time affair; one class only. After this class, the school was closed. Upon graduation each of us was issued an airplane, a reel of safety wire, a pair of needle-nose wire cutters, and a pocketknife. The knife we were told was to carve a propeller in case we broke one. Then we were shipped to the various areas where pilots and observation Cubs were in great need.

And Lt. Col. Jack L. Maranelli described what happened next:

Succeeding operations demonstrated magnificently the combat utility of the Cubs. The enemy, fighting a defensive campaign in which he was able to select his battleground, invariably chose to defend the high ground which assured him all the natural observation posts. Overcoming this advantage, our air observation posts provided target data for the artillery and intelligence on enemy operations.[2]

The effectiveness of using the Cubs against these German defensive strategies is apparent from the following account of one Grasshopper pilot and his observer during a mission in North Africa. They received orders to get up in the air in a hurry and locate some tanks that were bombarding our troops. When they got up over the front lines, they spotted the German guns flashing.

1. Paynee O. Lysne, "In That Box Is an Airplane," *Army Aviation* (Jan. 31, 1994): 65.
2. Jack L. Maranelli, "Army Aviation Surveys the Battle" *Army Information Digest* (Apr. 1950): 48.

Grasshoppers were the eyes in the sky for the field artillery.

They flew up to 2,000 feet and crossed behind the German lines so they could look down and adjust fire on the tanks. They knew they had to have a direct hit to knock out a tank. They radioed their coordinates back. Instantly, all hell broke loose. About 350 rounds were fired. The flak was so thick that they could hardly see anything. With antiaircraft fire tearing into their Cub, they dove for the Allied lines and dropped down to 800 feet. The plane was still under control, but the observer had sustained an injury from the flak. Once they reached the safety of their own territory and were back on the ground, they reported that they "tore the living hell" out of eight German tanks. This observation mission saved the lives of countless Allied troops and helped bring the war a bit closer to an end.

While these tactics did not improve our rapport with the Germans, they didn't hurt our efforts to improve relations with the citizens of the newly liberated territories. Not long after arriving in Tunisia, I used a schoolyard as my landing field. As I landed, the locals came up to my plane. I guess they thought something new was happening. One of the older men ran right into my prop before it had a chance to stop spinning. It put a gash in his shoulder several inches long. I got out of the plane, grabbed my first aid kit, and sprinkled some sulfa on the wound. I cleaned it out and patched it up. Fortunately, by this time I had learned about five months' worth of French, so I could understand a little of what they said to me.

The wounded man said, "This is different from the Germans. They would have turned around and shot me, but you got out of your airplane and bandaged me. We are in love with the Americans!"

· 5 ·

D-day Sicily

Since I had been guarding the French Moroccan border during the first five months of our invasion and occupation of North Africa, I had no actual combat duty to my credit, but I knew my time was coming. Our forces in the Tunisian war zone began preparations for another invasion. We didn't know exactly where it would be, but we each had our own thoughts on that subject. With the Nazi defeat in North Africa, next in line would, logically, be Sicily, and as the weeks passed there grew a general consensus developed that our preparations were being made for a summer campaign aimed against that island. The enemy had been fortifying Sicily for months with coastal guns and approximately 400,000 guerilla-tough, well-trained soldiers. They had fortifications on every high place, waiting for our men to land so they could eradicate every last one of them. But this mountainous island was the stepping-stone to the mainland. We had to take it.

Shortly after the Germans surrendered the naval base at Bizerte to the Allies, all landing vessels were ordered to proceed to Bizerte to be loaded for the invasion of Sicily. The city of Bizerte is located on the northern coast of Tunisia and adjacent to a large body of water called Lake Bizerte. A channel between the port and the lake had been built in early times and enlarged during the French occupation of Tunisia. When the Allies arrived they found that the Germans had reduced the city to rubble in their hasty retreat. But Bizerte had two strategic features that would assist the invasion: it had sufficient docks to accommodate the fleet of landing craft that needed to be outfitted, and, of the possible choices, it was the closest to the beaches of Sicily.

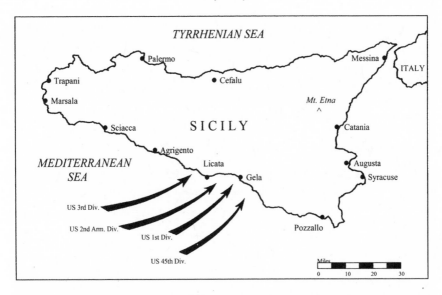

Col. Don E. Carleton, chief of staff of the U.S. Third Infantry Division, proposed to launch artillery spotter planes from the invasion fleet to fly over the beach area and report the actual situation as it happened to the flagship. They would also direct naval gunfire so that the field artillery could get ashore. There were no aircraft carriers available at this time for the Grasshoppers to be launched from, unlike the invasion of French Morocco, when three Grasshoppers had taken off from the aircraft carrier USS *Ranger.* Since the Third Division artillery spotter planes were to be in the air over the beach on D-day Sicily, the challenge was to improvise a way for the planes to take off without the use of an aircraft carrier. Sicily was too far for a Cub to fly from North Africa. The Cub had only two and a half hours' worth of fuel in its gas tank, and there was no place between Africa and Sicily to refuel.

Capt. Brenton A. Devol, Division Artillery Air Officer, had an idea and presented it to our division commander, who accepted it at once. The plane was to build a runway on the deck of one of our larger amphibious craft, have a plane take off on the morning of the invasion to locate enemy artillery fire and our own front lines, and keep headquarters advised of the landing conditions. It meant that whoever did this would have to take a chance on the invasion being successful, at least enough so that there would be a beachhead to land on, or else they would have to ditch in the water.

After evaluating all possible vessels in the fleet, the division commander agreed with Devol that the only prospect for launching an aircraft was the

LSTs revolutionized invasion strategies with their unique loading and unloading capabilities.

LST (Landing Ship Tank), which had enough forward deck to build a runway sufficient in length to get the Grasshopper to a takeoff speed of 65 mph.

After a short search, LST 386 was chosen and secured at Pier 24 for construction of the flight deck, which was to begin July 1. This vessel had been launched at Newport News Shipbuilding and Dry Dock Company in June 1942, and by early 1943 she had been in a convoy headed for the Mediterranean. At Bizerte she would undergo a transformation that would make her the world's first mini–aircraft carrier. Numerous other LSTs would be used for the same purpose in future invasions, but LST 386 was chosen to be the first. Her crew, commanded by Lt. Harold R. Fleck, USNR, displayed a sense of pride as they awaited the conversion.

My good friend Lt. (later Major) Francis A. Even (in the 10th Engineer Combat Battalion, U.S. Third Infantry Division), in his unpublished manuscript, "The Impromptu LST Aircraft Carriers of the Mediterranean in World War II,"[1] explains how things got organized:

> The engineer battalion commander, Lt. Col. Leonard L. Bingham, assigned the Battalion Intelligence Officer (S-2), Capt. Bertil V. Carlson, to the task, with orders to report to the Chief of Staff, who, with the help of the Division Artillery Air Officer, Capt. Brenton A. Devol, would outline the requirements. Capt. Devol had flown one of the three L-4s from the deck of the *Ranger* on the invasion of French Morocco, and presumably had already indicated probable feasibility. It remained simply to fit out LST 386, assigned by Adm. Connolly [Rear Adm. R. L. Connolly, Commander, Landing Craft and Bases, Northwest African Waters] for "carrier" duty, and to test it for the purpose.
>
> For the successful completion of this job in the short time remaining . . . he promised Capt. Carlson distinction in the form of promotion or decoration if the engineers could carry it off. Fortunately, "Bert" never took these blandishments seriously, but got right into the job, which he took up with the Battalion Executive Officer, Maj. Richard L. Earnhart, and the Battalion Operations Officer (S-3), Capt. Robert L. Petherick, as co-planners. Considering the available resources, they quickly decided upon a timber trestle down the centerline of the ship supporting a runway at bridge deck level that would extend forward from the superstructure to the bow, and just over the top of the 40mm gun tub on the bow.

The runway was to be 216 feet long and 10 feet wide, with a 1-foot sideboard on each side to help keep the plane on the runway. Even with Captain Devol's experience, flying off the improvised flight deck of this LST was entirely different from what the pilots were used to. With the invasion of Sicily scheduled for July 10, Captain Carlson had just a few days to get the runway built and tested.

On July 4 the transformed LST 386 was sent from her pier to the calm waters of Lake Bizerte. The test flight would be risky, but Captain Devol would never ask his men to do anything he had not tried himself. It was time for him to test the feasibility of taking off safely in an L-4 from the makeshift runway. A single Cub was placed on the runway of LST 386, which then moved to a

1. Francis A. Even, formerly Capt., 10th Engineer Combat Battalion, U.S. Third Infantry Division, WWII, unpublished manuscript, "The Impromptu LST Aircraft Carriers of the Mediterranean in World War II." Copyright 2000, 2001, F. A. Even, pp. 3, 4, with permission. The manuscript can be found at the U.S. Army Historical Institute, Carlisle Barracks, Pa., and the U.S. Army Aviation Museum, Fort Rucker, Ala., among other repositories.

Devol's Piper Cub awaits the historic test flight from the improvised runway built on the deck of LST 386 at Lake Bizerte, July 4, 1943, before heading off at full throttle. Courtesy Peter T. Millaras.

Success! Captain Devol proves that Piper Cubs will be able to take part in the imminent invasion of Sicily by piloting the first plane to take off successfully from the deck of an LST. Courtesy Peter T. Millaras.

remote area of the lake. The ship headed at full speed into the wind. The plane took off from the runway—with room to spare.

Even continues his account of the event:

> It appeared that Capt. Devol's plane had edged to the starboard side of the runway by the time of liftoff.... The edges of the runway [in the photo] are notched by the amount of the ... offset of the airport runway grating sections where joined by their designed connectors. Whether the engineers simply had not finished their work, or whether as the result of Capt. Devol's takeoff experience, the notches in the runway edges were covered by slanted-plank curbs when we boarded three days later for the crossing to Licata, Sicily. The curbs would presumably alert the pilot if his plane should stray too dangerously from the centerline stripe.[2]

The plan had worked perfectly. Devol's successful takeoff was proof that the plan could work and that others might expect the same success. LST 386 and her crew returned to port with the full realization that the real test would take place in hostile territory under heavy fire and in all likelihood, in unfavorable weather conditions.

The next thing to do was get volunteer pilots. The general decided to have two planes take off instead of one-if one happened to crash on takeoff or was shot down, there was still the possibility that the other one would succeed. He asked for volunteers, and three of us stepped forward to accept the challenge. Lt. Oliver P. Board and I were chosen.

On July 6 Bob Hope and his entertainment troupe, including Frances Langford, were at Bizerte to entertain the GIs. They had just finished their show when an enemy air raid struck the dock area. German "chandelier" flares lit up the surface of the lake and the landing ships that were docked there. LST 386 was still berthed at Pier 24, and the flares had illuminated the white stripe that was painted down the runway to aid the pilots when taking off. Seeing it, the German aircraft attacked. The gun crew was positioned at the end of the runway, and the prominent line made it easy to strafe the LST from one end to the other, killing two members of the gun crew and wounding six others, including the gunnery officer.

The ship itself was not seriously damaged, and later that day she was moved to Pier 27, where vital cargo for the invasion was to be loaded. For three hours

2. Ibid. pp. 9, 10.

July 8, 1943. LST 386 stands loaded and ready for the invasion of Sicily. Notice the Cub camouflaged on the runway. Courtesy Peter T. Millaras.

she took on vehicles, troops, and the four Piper Cubs. The first two, one of them my *Maggie the Faithful,* were positioned nose to tail at the end of the runway. The tail of *Maggie* was lashed to the deck boat rail to immobilize her until the time came for action. The two other L-4s were located just off the flight deck, ready to be hauled into takeoff position if needed.

Even's unit was assigned to ride LST 386 from Bizerte to the invasion site at Licata in Sicily. They would witness the success of this historic early-morning launching of the two Cubs from an LST—the first ever.

We boarded the LST, found our quarters, and carefully inspected our airplanes. This was going to be my first experience in live combat, and, needless to say, I was very anxious. Fortunately, I was comforted by some of my fellow pilots. "This is it!" they reminded me in a consoling manner. "This is what you trained for during those days at Fort Sill."

We made all the necessary preparations. We got our maps out to familiarize ourselves with the terrain we were to cover and studied all the possible gun positions.

Lieutenant Board and I were often teased about being "the suicide twins." I was scared stiff at times thinking about what could happen. The name stuck with Board and me for some time after that because of some of the fool things we would do later in northern Sicily just to get a shot at Jerry.

We knew that this was a journey of no return—our runway was designed for takeoff only. Heaven only knew where we would be able to land. We prayed that our troops would take enough of the beach in that first two and a half hours of battle to afford us a place to land our Cubs to refuel.

Weather conditions were not very favorable as our ship left the pier. We headed toward the island, just off the tip of the Italian boot. Sicily, a beautiful, romantic land, was soon to be ravaged and torn by the ugly, evil, angry jaws of war.

The Mediterranean was tossing and churning, as if warning us not to proceed. But proceed we did. We soon would acquire much respect and admiration for this magnificent sea as a haven from the dangers of our mission. Enemy gunfire would often force us to fly out over its expansive surface where we could evade and outdistance the deadly projectiles sent our way.

The night before the invasion was a windy one. We thought our planes would be blown off the runway. Dozens of times that evening and during night we went out to see if the wind had carried them away. By early morning, as we neared the shore, the wind had subsided.

July 10, 1943, D-day, H-hour plus one—our moment of takeoff was at hand. The sky was filled with ack-ack, both ours and the enemy's. Our guns were bombarding the beach installations, and they were bombarding our landing craft.

Just as it was light enough for a takeoff, we asked the skipper to head his LST at full speed into the wind. Lieutenant Board gunned his engine, looked back at me with a grin, and took off. As he neared the end of the runway, the ship lurched, and for a moment I thought he was going off the starboard side, but he kicked the left rudder soon enough, and off to the port side he turned. Immediately after clearing the runway, he sank out of sight. For a terrifying moment everyone watching his takeoff expected to hear him crash, but miraculously he rose up as swiftly as he had fallen, nose pointed skyward, then headed directly for the beach.

He made it there safely; however, for some unknown reason, his radio didn't work. Because he couldn't communicate, he landed on the beach close to the water, where our troops had already established themselves. Relieved that he was at least not in enemy hands, he tried to repair his radio but was unsuccessful. As he watched troops and equipment pour from the landing ships and move forward, he felt great disappointment that he had not been able to fulfill his mission.

Next was me. A crewman and I put my plane in place and, asking the help of the good Lord, I climbed in. The crewman cranked the prop, and I nervously revved up the engine. I waited until the vessel was steady for a moment; before she had a chance to roll and pitch too much, I was on my way down the runway. Before I reached the end of it, I was in the air. A perfect headwind had given me the lift I so desperately needed. Over the bow I went, not knowing exactly what was going to happen next.

Lieutenant Even was also on hand to witness these historic takeoffs. His account confirms the dramatic events that catapulted Lieutenant Board and me into the mouth of hell:

The forward plane had been turned around to face forward. Its prop was turning as its engine warmed with pilot Lt. Oliver P. "Woody" Board at the controls. He revved up the engine, standing on the brakes, and rolled forward with the tail lifted on the prop wash. The plane rolled off the end of the runway, disappearing over the bow, as viewed from the bridge deck, and causing momentary consternation until it rose into view again, climbing, and turned for shore.

The second plane, now fully on the runway with engine turning over and warming, Lt. Julian W. "Bill" Cummings at the controls, similarly roared to life and rolled forward, with tail elevated to give the pilot full view of the center stripe of the runway, and rose into the air even before it reached the end of the runway.

Silently, we wished them both good luck as everyone realized that they were committed, and very much on their own.[3]

Just as I made the turn toward the beach, a timed-fuse shell exploded off the starboard bow of the ship. I didn't know where it had come from, but one of my buddies later said that after I had cleared the area a second round went over the ship. A coastal defense gun at the entrance to the harbor at Licata had opened fire on LST 386. Even the inexperienced crew knew the third round would be a direct hit. I guess everyone was nervous waiting for that third round, but my buddy said that the ship's lookout spotted the guns and quickly radioed their location to the flagship. The shore battery was knocked out by our naval guns, and LST 386 and its crew were safe for the moment.

I flew down low over the water, weaving in and out among our landing craft, waving to let them know that I was an American observation plane and not an enemy. I remembered how Capt. Ford Alcorn had been mistakenly shot down by our own guns.

3. Ibid. p. 16.

D-day, Sicily. Bill's takeoff from the deck of LST 386 makes history.

When I called in to the flagship and told them I was in the air, they radioed back and told me to see how things were on the beach. Our boys had landed there only one hour before. I climbed to 1,500 feet and flew in toward the beach.

The boys were really taking a shelling. It was my first sight of our own men being blown up and wounded by enemy fire. I was being baptized into combat flying. Time after time I would see shells come in on them, and every so often a variable-time shell would come very close to my plane. I put my helmet on over my earphones; it was uncomfortable, but it gave me the feeling that if fragments did come my way, the metal shell might stave off some of them.

I radioed in what I had seen, and they said to do all I could to locate the guns. I flew in over the beach and inland about three miles. There, right alongside a small railroad station, I saw puffs of smoke belching out of four enemy artillery locations. That was just what I was looking for. I was so excited that when I called in the coordinates of the position to the Navy, I read them backwards. However, I corrected the mistake immediately, and the Navy gave the enemy a real shelling. No more German shells hit that beach that morning.

The same thing was occurring in the eastern extremity of our sector. Just as I arrived I saw a shell land right at the open bow doors of an LST, doing considerable damage. I couldn't locate the enemy guns inland, so I flew further down the beach. A couple of miles from where the shelling occurred, I saw four more puffs of smoke coming from a knoll that ran down to the sea. I had flown right over the guns before noticing them. They had machine guns alongside the artillery emplacements, yet they did not shoot at me. They must have thought I was one of their own observation planes, for I did not see any ack-ack or (though there were quite a few in the air that morning) enemy planes heading right at me. They probably couldn't understand how one of our light planes could fly over from Africa with as little range as our planes had.

As I flew down the beach to the location of a force of Army Rangers, I saw them advancing up a hill that was being shelled by our ships. The boys had made good progress. I called in the information and the Navy ceased firing in that sector to keep from hitting the Rangers. I located our lines as best I could and reported them in to headquarters. Having used up all but ten minutes of my fuel supply, I decided to land. I had, flying from beach to beach, spotted a nice green patch where the Rangers had gone in. I headed for that spot and started in for a landing. As I made my low drag, I noticed a barbed-wire fence right across the middle. No landing here—a crackup because of a fence would be bad at that moment. But I had to refuel to finish my job. I climbed up a couple of hundred feet and headed in over a small hill; up near the road I spotted some of our infantry crossing a small flat spot. I buzzed them, and as they got out of the way, I landed. I knew that by going where our boys had already safely walked, I wouldn't be landing on any personnel mines, as had Lieutenant Stevens in Tunisia.

I got out of my plane and walked down to the beach to procure gasoline from one of our vehicles that was unloading. There was plenty of war activity going on all around. Most of the GIs didn't know who I was or what I was doing there. However, the driver of the truck showed no hesitation when I told him who I was and said that in order to continue my mission I would have to beg some gasoline for my observation plane. It was only a short while until my plane was refueled and I was on my way, very grateful to that cooperative truck driver for the fuel he so willingly provided. Immediately after I took off, I found plenty more enemy activity, which kept me busy reporting my observations to the flagship.

I had spent nearly the entire day flying behind enemy lines to find German gun nests. It amused me to recall what we had been taught at Field Artillery School back at Fort Still. They had warned us *never* to fly over enemy lines or even *close* to them.

During the pre-invasion period, many of the men had contracted malaria. I was no exception. In fact, I had come down with a case of dysentery as well. My weight had dropped considerably. So, I was not in the best health at the time of the invasion of Sicily. (Several weeks later I found myself spending one day in the field hospital for every two days in the air.)

As I flew around our sector looking for more targets of opportunity to turn over to our artillery, dysentery hit me. I looked around and soon found a beautiful green pasture just right for an "emergency" landing. I turned into the wind and landed a little uphill toward the west. There were no animals to threaten me, so I quickly opened the cockpit door, jumped out, and immediately dropped my pants.

Just as I stooped down, I heard a roar off to the east. I looked over my shoulder, and there it was—a Stuka dive-bomber coming toward me at a low strafing angle. I couldn't miss those gull-shaped wings and fixed landing gear. I was a direct target for this joker, and I didn't relish the idea of being a sitting duck, so to speak. I grabbed at my pants, pulling them up as best as I could as I ran to the right of my airplane. Some twenty yards in that direction was a lone tree with a trunk about two and a half feet in diameter. I arrived behind it just in the nick of time. Machine gun bullets began to tear up the ground on either side of the trunk. That pilot was out to get *me*, not my airplane. I watched him head west and kept my eyes on him to see if he would make another pass at me or my little L-4. But he continued heading west. Then I heard the sound of aircraft again, and as I peered out around the tree trunk, I saw two P-51 Mustang pursuit planes coming fast and heading west.

If he had been smart, he could have destroyed my aircraft. But he was too busy trying to get me and, in the process, muffed the whole deal. But he did nearly scare the dysentery out of me! I was just grateful for that beautiful big tree and those gorgeous P-51s. I went back to the air with a great sense of relief that I had survived this scary episode.

As this longest day of my life continued, I witnessed many horrifying scenes. Some of my pilot buddies and good friends were departing from the vessels that had transported us from Africa to the shores of Sicily; some of the disassembled Grasshoppers were unloaded through the gaping bow doors of LSTs and placed in trucks from the Third Division motor pool to be delivered to appropriate places where the pilots could assemble their airplanes and prepare for action. The beach was a mass of confusion, but people and vehicles all seemed to be going in one direction. Foremost in every mind seemed to be, "Get off the beach, forthwith!" The drivers of the trucks also seemed to have only one thought, to dump their loads and escape the confusion.

Not everyone was able to escape. I saw one bomb explode at the bow doors of an LST, disrupting the unloading of anything from that vessel for some time. From my aerial view, I saw GIs wounded and some killed. The sight from the sky was horrifying. I knew that if anyone was in a position to help, it was me, so I continued doing everything I could to locate the enemy and, with the help of the Navy, eradicate them.

The day was a most unusual one. It was probably not much different from any day in combat for most of the GIs, but this was my first combat mission. As daylight vanished and darkness crept in, I landed *Maggie* not far from the beach and prepared for night. As I lay my weary body down, bombs and shells exploded in the near distance. I mused on the happenings of that day. I was never a hunter. I didn't like to kill anything. Yet this very day many had died, many had been injured, and countless lives had been saved because of the accomplishment of my mission. I felt a pang of sorrow for the enemy and a mighty feeling of "well done" for our GIs. Fatigue overcame me, and with a prayer of thankfulness in my heart, I fell asleep.

Sometime later—it seemed like mere minutes—my sleep was interrupted by a terrible outburst of guns and exploding bombs. For a frantic moment I thought the sky was falling. Planes were dropping something. Could it be paratroopers? All I could tell was that our Navy was shooting at whatever they were as they drifted earthward. After a while that nightmare seemed to subside somewhat.

Again overcome by bewilderment and fatigue, I settled down to catch some badly needed sleep. I felt weak, alone, and helpless. As I closed my eyes, the world seemed to be spinning around me, and visions of the horrors of that day enveloped my mind. "Oh my God," I cried, "what have I done?" Almost before those thoughts escaped my lips, I knew that I was not alone, that I had been guided in my actions of the day, and that the lives which had been saved outweighed everything else. A calmness came over me, and with a prayer on my lips to survive that night, I again drifted into slumber, knowing that someone greater than I had brought me through this hellish day.

Another fortunate survivor of that terrifying day was my close buddy, Lt. Alfred W. "Dutch" Schultz, who was in the third wave to hit the beach on D-day Sicily. His Piper Cub, *Janey*, had been neatly stacked in the bed of a two-and-a-half-ton cargo truck. Her fuselage was in the truck's steel bed, her wings were strapped to the side of the truck, and the tools for assembling her were in and around her disassembled parts.

Two hours after the invasion commenced, Dutch's Piper Cub was on the beach, and he was frantically trying to find an appropriate place to assemble her. Amid all the exploding gas dumps, the rattling of the .50-caliber weapons, the rolling thunder of 40 mm antiaircraft guns, the continual downpour of bombs, the movement of people, trucks, and war machines, and the confusion of such entangled surroundings, Dutch could hardly believe it would be possible to assemble Janey. Just trying to find someone to hold the wings while he secured them to her seemed impossible. Everyone was totally engaged in getting to where they were assigned and saving their own necks, ducking bullets and moving vehicles.

By midmorning Janey was unloaded from her cramped quarters on the borrowed truck. The driver of the truck, Corporal Bostrom, a Third Division motor pool driver, had only one thing in mind—to dump *Janey*, Corporal Coral, and Dutch and escape from this pandemonium, which he did.

Dutch's orders were very clear. He was to make Janey flyable and wait on the beach until his observer showed up. The observer, in turn, was to find an appropriate place to land. But the day was fading, with no observer, and Dutch's airplane was still unflyable.

The frustration and confusion of that miserable day had taken its toll on Dutch, so Corporal Coral suggested they build a shelter out of the mountain of C-ration cases stacked on the beach and line it with straw from a nearby stack. He figured out that this crude fort would possibly deflect any shrapnel coming their way, and they could at least get some sort of rest on makeshift mattresses. Moments later, while they were discussing the events of the day in their new shelter, all hell broke loose. A barrage from our ships started to roll toward them, and soon every gun in the area was sending balls of burning steel skyward. The planes overhead weren't dropping bombs; they were dropping American paratroopers. The Navy was shooting at the parachutes as they drifted slowly to the beach.

At last it stopped. Schultz and Coral had witnessed the complete disruption of a landing of the American 82d Airborne Division. The battered remains of the 82d returned to North Africa. Horrified and amazed, Dutch and Coral realized that their crude C-ration fort had saved their lives. Maybe the next day would afford a semblance of sanity.[4]

Following D-day Sicily at Licata, on July 28 orders were delivered to me to report to division headquarters in the field. I had a feeling it was about something pertaining to the volunteer mission I had flown, but there wasn't anything in my orders to make that clear. The orders simply said to "report immediately."

I trudged to headquarters. Had I done something wrong? Had I messed up in any way during that dreadful invasion day? Would my folks and Maggie be proud of me or ashamed? I consoled myself with a belief that everything I had done during that day had been with the intent to help our men survive the barrage of bullets belching from the German guns. It seemed that our men were going headlong into that fortified island. Those guns had to be stopped.

As I drew near headquarters, I decided that whatever was waiting for me I would take. With no clue as to what was about to happen, I stood for a moment at the entrance to see if I could tell what was going on. I heard muffled voices engaged in conversation, but there were too many to single out any familiar one. I entered slowly, to attract as little attention as possible. About a dozen officers were standing around, and as I stepped in all eyes turned toward me. Then a loud cheer and spontaneous applause threw me back on my heels. I received an overwhelming hero's welcome. My superior officers were all there, with hands outstretched to congratulate me. I could hardly believe

4. Alfred W. Schultz, with Kirk Neff, *Janey: A Little Plane in a Big War* (Middleton, Conn.: Southfarm, 1998).

C O N F I D E N T I A L

HEADQUARTERS SEVENTH ARMY
APO #758, U. S. ARMY

21 July 1943.

SUBJECT: Award of the Distinguished Service Cross.

TO   : 2nd Lieut. Julian W. Cummings, 10th F. A. Battalion.

1. Under the provisions of AR 600-45 as amended, a
Distinguished Service Cross is awarded to 2nd Lieutenant JULIAN
W. CUMMINGS, F. A.

JULIAN W. CUMMINGS, Second Lieutenant, F.A., 10th
Field Artillery Battalion. For extraordinary heroism in action.
During the assault phase of the landing near Gela, Sicily, on
10 July 1943, Lt. Cummings, Battalion Artillery Air Officer, took
off in a piper cub plane in advance of the required time, and
under incessant fire, from an improvised runway on the deck of
an LST, to spot and report positions of enemy artillery then laying
highly effective fire on beaches being used to land elements of
the Armed forces for 2 1/2 hours with utter disregard for personal
safety. In addition he located and reported the progress of our
front line to the Force Commander. Lt. Cummings landed on a coastal roadway near our Armed forces, refueled from vehicles, and
again took to the air to continue his mission. Lt. Cumming's
initiative, resourcefulness and extraordinary bravery under fire
to accomplish an urgent mission contributed materially to the
success of the operation. The distinguished service rendered by
Lt. Cummings reflects the finest traditions of the military service.
Residence: Salt Lake City, Utah.

G S Patton Jr.

G. S. PATTON, JR.,
Lieutenant General, U. S. Army,
Commanding.

- 1 -

C O N F I D E N T I A L

Bill's Distinguished Service Cross award.

what was happening. My commanding officer, Gen. L. K. Truscott Jr., beckoned me to come forward. I snapped to attention and stepped up to face him as he took a document and a medal from an aide standing by.

I heard only vague snatches of words as he read the citation: "By command of Lt. Gen. George Patton . . . for saving the lives of 15,000 men . . . for outstanding bravery . . . for extraordinary bravery under fire. . . . The distinguished service rendered . . . reflects the finest traditions of the military service."

As the Distinguished Service Cross was pinned on my uniform shirt, I was overcome with emotion. Never had I dreamed my actions would be called heroic—a little daring perhaps, but being a hero had never been my motive. After I recovered somewhat from all these accolades, I was then asked to drink a toast with the division and corps commanders. I had never drunk a toast using alcohol in my life, and I certainly wasn't going to start now, since the consumption of any alcoholic beverage was against my religious upbringing. But to refuse could be interpreted as a refusal to acknowledge the great honor just paid me by those I respected as my military leaders. I was torn between a commitment to my most fervent moral convictions and my respect for the country I loved.

Summoning what seemed like more bravery than I had needed at the beachhead on July 10, I turned to the commander and whispered, "Drinking liquor is totally against my religion, sir."

"Oh, that's perfectly all right," he whispered back. "Here's a glass of water. It'll work just as well." Much relieved, I thanked the commander for his kind and sensitive gesture and was grateful that a moral dilemma had not caused me to show disrespect to either my country or my God.

At the end of the celebration they gave me my copy of the citation from General Patton, and I walked back to my quarters feeling just a little braver than before. I didn't get much sleep that night, with the importance of the day's event finally settling in. I wrote letters to Maggie and my parents the next day to let them know of the award.

The success of my mission on D-day Sicily demonstrated the value of artillery air observation planes in combat. Our planes were so important to the forces in Sicily that one of the commanding generals stated that if it hadn't been for the Cubs, the Sicilian campaign would have lasted another two or three weeks. As it was, it took the Allies thirty-eight days to defeat the enemy in Sicily.

·6·

The Sicilian Campaign

After our forces captured Licata, they pushed northward toward Agrigento. Their advance was slow and hazardous, with every hilltop capped by a German fortress. My job was to locate each one. During the assault I was in the air adjusting fire for my battalion when I saw several fighter planes coming right at me. I yelled over the radio, "Are those enemy or friendly planes?" By the time I got the answer back that they were friendly, I had dived down over a small village and nearly took the top off a steeple. Finally I recognized them as our P-51s, so I again breathed more easily.

We Grasshoppers were always being shot at, but since we were able to outmaneuver most enemy guns, we had little evidence to prove it. So there were a few skeptics on the ground who questioned the validity of our claims that we were frequent targets of ground fire. While flying near Agrigento I had been fired upon by small arms and machine guns. Upon returning, I told some of the other officers about it. One officer didn't believe me, so I asked him if he would like a hop over enemy lines. He said yes, so I took him with me. About fifteen minutes out, we heard a few cracks of rifle shots and also saw a few tracers just off the nose of the plane. The officer said, "That's enough—take me back. I believe your story now."

The push was on to reach the city of Palermo as quickly as possible. On the way, my air section stopped near the little town of Buigio to prepare a new landing strip. In the battalion's haste to reach Palermo, they bypassed our airstrip without realizing it. Later that day my mechanic and a Grasshopper pilot, Sgt. James T. Smith, found themselves the only Americans left in Buigio. They were kings for the day, they said. Sergeant Smith even turned loose some of the

Sergeant Smith sitting on a downed German fighter plane.

political prisoners who had been left behind in the town jail by the Germans in their hasty retreat. The residents of Buigio would never forget Smith, who for that brief day brought a new kind of joy and excitement to their little village.

After a few brief days of appreciated rest in Palermo, our division was called back into line to replace the "Oklahoma Thunderbirds" (the Forty-fifth Division) east of Palermo, on the north coast. Though we were informed of the approximate location of German troops and their ragged lines from rugged seacoast to the high mountaintops, we Grasshoppers still preferred to maneuver our little "Maytag Messerschmitts" out over Jerryland to get firsthand information on their actual location. All of us were still quite green in wanting to find the fighting Germans in our Piper Cubs. Fortunately, the Jerries were still novices when it came to making clay pigeons out of us.

Captain Devol and I took off in his Cub in a cloud of dust, skimming over the tops of some halftracks parked at the end of our too-short runway. Out over the blue Mediterranean and up the coastline we flew, weaving in and out of ravines and over dusty roads until we reached the widespread delta of a dry riverbed. By this time none of our vehicles could be seen on the road. In fact, not even a slow-trudging member of one of our forward reconnaissance parties could be found. It looked too quiet down there. We circled out over the water to get a prolonged look at the delta and a blown-out bridge. So far our G-2 (staff intelligence) information was correct. Back over the delta we flew, but as we started up the coast again a machine gun fired at us from below and to our rear. Captain Devol made an abrupt left turn and headed out to sea, weaving and nosing down to pick up more speed. I turned to the rear of the plane and watched tracers come closer and closer, but soon we were out of range. The magnificent Mediterranean had once again become our protector. Luckily for us, the enemy was accustomed to shooting at our faster brothers, the Mustangs and twin-boomed P-38 Lightnings.

I marked their location on my map and turned on the radio. We had found Jerry and meant to liquidate him in a quick reprisal. I called, but no answer. Fine thing. Jerry had just about shot us out of the sky, and nobody was riding the radio waves to assist us in exterminating Hitler's little helpers.

We flew back to the strip muttering oaths of disgust. After a quick and pointed phone call, we went back into the air, fearing only that Jerry had been smart enough to move his guns and lose us the chance of sending more Germans to Valhalla. But he hadn't been. "Base point 550 right 600 short," I hastily called in to Fire Direction Center.

"On the way," came the answer a few minutes later.

"Beautiful! Bull's-eye! Fire for effect," I called back.

By this time Jerries were running for cover.

"Fire for effect," came a quick reply, and the next rounds arrived just in time to catch a handful of men running across the road to an old dilapidated stone house. It was too late. The timed fire had mowed them down like raking machine-gun fire. One more lesson was learned of Jerry's ways. Instead of moving, he waited. This gave us time to fly back and repay him for trying to shoot us out of the sky. Luckily, we had had the Mediterranean to fly out over; otherwise we might never have made it back.

In the battle for San Fratello we had to sweat out flying through trajectories of our own weapons on every mission we flew. Luckily, none of us was ever hit by our own shells…this time.

At Coronia our division command post had been shelled rather frequently, and nobody seemed able to find those guns. One day, as I was up looking for one of our battalions, I was evidently hidden against a mountain to my rear when suddenly I saw four gun blasts in a draw on the other side of the hill, where Coronia was located. They wouldn't have fired and given away their position had they known I was there. I immediately radioed back the position of those guns, and we placed a concentration of artillery fire all over that area. Those German guns were quiet from that time on. From there on to Messina, we were continually finding enemy positions.

Flying over enemy lines was one way of finding enemy positions, and it was also a way to silence them. If we spotted the Germans, we would shell them so heavily that they would be silenced permanently, and they knew it. They had finally gotten wise to our tactics; when they spotted us, they would stop shooting. We knew what they were doing, so we started constant patrol. This helped out a lot, for usually, as long as one of our planes was in the air, the enemy could not or would not fire. After a short time they got tired of our constant patrol and decided to retaliate by sending out fighter planes with the prime mission of shooting us down. That didn't stop us Grasshoppers; if we saw them coming at us, we would make a tight turn and outmaneuver them.

On the north coast of Sicily I would often fly behind enemy lines by way of the Mediterranean Sea. At times they would let me get away with it, and at other times they would shoot at me. Out of twenty-seven missions in Sicily, they shot at me twenty times with ack-ack, machine guns, and small arms. I was never hit during any of those flights.

On one occasion we had been fired on by the Germans for a couple of days. most of the shells had been landing in the Division Command Post. We had no success locating the guns. I happened to be up on a reconnaissance mission with a captain trying to locate an infantry battalion that was up in the hills. We had been up an hour and a half and, as before, were camouflaged by the higher mountains to the south, so the Germans evidently couldn't see our Cub in the air. This, they thought, was the time to lay some more shells in our backyard. Four flashes followed by four bluish-white puffs of smoke went out from a draw, just a hundred yards south of the highway next to the sea.

"Beautiful," I said to the captain. "That's what we've been looking for these last two days. Just watch me pay them back for what they did to us." I noted the landmarks and the exact bend in the dry streambed the fire had come from and went back to refuel and to get an observer trained to read the map coordinates and adjust fire. A half-hour later those Jerries wished they'd never fired. We poured out almost 500 rounds into that area. Proof of the effectiveness of the fire was evident later. When the GIs took the area, they found one of the guns still there. It was so badly damaged that the Germans had not even salvaged it, as they usually did. There was also great evidence of more destruction, such as wrecked vehicles and other equipment strewn around.

On another occasion, for more than a day one of our road junctions had been receiving interdiction fire (meant to stop movement) from the Germans, and we couldn't seem to find where it was coming from. That morning I was up just looking over the area, waiting for a fire mission from my battalion, when I sighted a tank on the road just behind a little knoll. I immediately radioed in and asked if we had any tanks in that vicinity.

They said we had none there at all. I took another good look and had just made a sharp turn above them when up came some nice red tracers just off the nose of my plane. I told myself they couldn't possibly be friendly, but I wanted to take a better look from a little safer distance. This time I took a good reading and noticed that the tank was on the enemy side of a blown-out bridge and that there were no tank tracks around the blown section, so it had not come from our side of the bridge. I also noticed that the tank was on the enemy side of the knoll and that it was in full view of the enemy but not of us. We had some jeeps approaching up the road in that direction. If they tried to get around that hill, Jerry would ambush them. I got permission to shoot beyond the tanks and gradually bring the fire back down on them. By shortening this range, there would be no danger of hitting any of our men. The mission was fired, and the tank took off up the road like a scared rabbit. Thirty seconds later a truck with a towed gun followed them in good order. Although the shells had missed the enemy, some had landed very close, and the interdiction fire on our road junction had been silenced.

I had some very good success in locating and helping to knock out or scare off tanks lying in ambush for our reconnaissance vehicles and patrols. All of us Grasshoppers enjoyed chasing enemy tanks around. They would hide behind a tree line, thinking that they were hidden from view, but when we would lay shells on top of them, they would think a little differently and take off deeper back into Jerryland.

I have often wondered about the change in my thinking. The things I had to do during combat were totally contrary to my habits in civilian life. Before the war, I would never have thought of harming another human being. Yet with an enemy at our back door with every intention of destroying everything honorable that we believed in, my thinking became, "Get him before he gets any of us." It's strange how actual war forces one into an entirely different position and way of thinking. Yet every one of us on the front lines longed to bring an end to this horrible nightmare and return to our homeland and loved ones.

My silent prayer before takeoff always seemed to set things right and invite a special guardian angel to be with me. At all times I felt the assurance of this protection. Divine intervention played an important part in my military combat activities.

One day during our Sicilian operation, I was heading for our battalion command post when I was diverted into another direction to see something or someone else. This delayed me about twenty minutes. Its reason was unimportant as far as my work was concerned; however, the delay may have saved my life.

When I arrived at our battalion command post, I saw a very bloody scene. The telephone operator lay dead by the side of his equipment. Lieutenant Markala, an officer assigned to the command post, was being carried out on a stretcher. He had blood all over his body. He gave me a weak smile, for we were good buddies. There were also several others in a similar condition.

I don't remember what about this horrible experience diverted me for the critical twenty minutes. I say it was divine intervention. That special priesthood blessing I received in the Salt Lake Temple before going into combat had again proved true in the war. The promise that I would return home without shedding a drop of my blood gave me the courage to volunteer for the suicide flight in the invasion of Sicily. I flew a total of 485 patrol and combat missions in the war. I was shot at many times, but I was never the recipient of a Purple Heart.

I have a difficult time understanding how any soldier could face the horrors of war without believing in and relying on a power greater than himself. I am grateful for my belief. It has made me physically and spiritually strong, and it has carried me through the most terrifying moments of my life.

For five weeks after the beginning of the Sicilian campaign, we and our allies stormed enemy pillboxes, seized Italian and German airfields, and occupied towns as enemy troops retreated northward to Messina. This was the last escape port to the mainland of Italy. By mid-August Messina, too, was ours; the enemy had fled, leaving behind some 135,000 stragglers who had missed the evacuation ships and thousands more dead. Sicily had indeed been a stepping-stone to the European continent, to Rome, to the surrender of Mussolini's fascist government, and to the occupation of Italy. But this was just the beginning—Germany and France were next.

Predictably, only nine days after the end of the Sicilian campaign, I was transferred to the Italian invasion zone, with instructions to prepare myself for another Grasshopper "infestation."

· 7 ·

Invasion of Italy

After about four weeks of badly needed rest camp, we headed for Italy. Salerno was our goal, but by the time we got there the situation was pretty well in hand. We took over our sector and started toward Naples, flying our L-4s. At Acerno we were being held up by a few gun positions. The Germans had gotten wise to us and found that if they shot ack-ack at us, we would stay behind that fire. This day, I was up adjusting on the enemy gun position, and they shot one round up at me. That was enough for me. I used that as a marker and stayed right behind it, but I still finished my adjustment on the enemy guns.

I remember that it was either Captain Maranelli or Goodwin who thought it would be a good idea to fly on moonlit nights. We could at least stop some of the interdiction firing. Johnny Oswald and I picked up on the idea, and we would take off at night with no lights. Naturally, you couldn't have any lights up near the front, so we would take off down the strip, which you could see fairly well on a moonlit night. We could also see the mountain around us; we would come in close to it, where we could be heard but not be seen. The enemy wouldn't fire at us, because they knew the minute they fired we could locate their positions and retaliate with our own artillery.

There were many roads leading inland out of the town of Avellino, located in the province of Campania, and the Germans had done such a perfect job of demolition, bridge blowing, and road blocking that it was difficult for the engineers to determine which road net would be the best for ground troops to follow. It was up to us Cub pilots in daylight to map from the air which road net could be repaired most easily and which bridges would be easiest to bypass. This saved the engineers days of work, and time.

Bill and Capt. Lee Isaacs (right) at Volturno River, Italy.

On the way to Monteforte one day, I was again uncertain of our front line, but as I flew north I soon found out where it was, for the German demolition crews started firing up at me. All the way through Italy we saw plenty of the destructive work of the German army. The little village of San Clemente was blown to bits for no good reason. The natives told us that the Germans had blown the buildings up with no warning and that many of their friends and families had been killed. The same was true for Acerno and many other villages.

As we were getting ready for the Volturno River crossing, I had to reconnoiter for an observation point. Capt. Lee Isaacs and I flew down low, just behind a hill overlooking the river. We thought that this village and valley were inhabited by our infantry, but as we flew about 300 feet over the fox- holes, we could hear the machine pistols shooting at us. We decided then and there that they were not friendly troops but enemy. The Volturno River would give us many experiences before we finally got past it.

Smitty, one of our sergeant pilots, was shot down by a Messerschmitt that had been dive-bombing a pontoon bridge on the Volturno. However, he was fortunate enough to receive only a few scratches. Smitty (sometimes "Jimmy," really Staff Sgt. James T. Smith) had named his plane both *Wilma,* after his wife, and *Elaine,* after his baby daughter. Smitty always said, "We're all in this plane together—me and my family!" Another time as Smitty walked toward his *Wilma Elaine* Piper Cub, the command warned him again to be on the lookout for Messerschmitt ME-109s. All day they had been drifting across the lines, sometimes three and sometimes six. Smitty remembered that he and his *Wilma Elaine* had been chased by an ME that very morning. He taxied down the cow pasture, dodging the shell craters that the enemy had left the night before, bombing the area for an hour or more.

Wilma Elaine climbed at about 50 mph, seemed to stand still, then headed off into the valley of Mignano. In this area an American division had been gaining ground in a German-held sector. Smitty was flying behind the Ger- man line at about 3,000 feet when suddenly *Wilma Elaine* lifted slightly and then dropped. Over to the American side he went, in as big a hurry as his slow-moving plane could manage.

Sergeant Smith's duties were to keep the plane on the target and watch out for MEs. He knew the MEs always came out of the sun, so he never kept his back to the sun for very long. He watched for our own ground flak, which would tell him there was enemy aircraft around. He watched for any ground shadows that didn't match that of his *Wilma Elaine.* He also looked for vapor trails, and there ahead of him, pointing westward beyond the sea, he saw some—six U.S. fighters.

As Smitty watched, the fighters came out of the sun and went into a bomb- ing dive. The bombs dripped like gray tears off the nose of those American A- 36 Invaders and hit a road intersection north of Mignano. Smitty then flew close to Mount Lunga, where for several days the Germans had held the high peak and the Yanks the lower, east peak. The entire mountain was shrouded in a cloak of smoke from exploding shells. But Smitty knew the Germans were too deep in their foxholes to send any arrows of death in his direction. Suddenly Smitty made a diving turn, headed down, down, then pulled out and ducked into a mountain valley. Something above had drawn flak from

Staff Sgt. "Smitty" Smith (left) and Bill in front of Smitty's Cub, Wilma Elaine.

those below. Shortly after, *Wilma Elaine* hedgehopped back to her cow pasture runway.

Smitty was an experienced pilot. He had flown before the war and by this time had fifty-six combat missions to his credit. Experienced as he was, he was scared of Messerschmitts and was always on the lookout for them. That very morning one had come close enough to open up with its guns. Just a few weeks before, he had had to make a crash landing to get away from one of those Jerry deathtraps.

Later, during rest camp, Smitty took a GI up for a ride. Unaware that they were being tailed, he set about giving his buddy a tour of the area. From behind an ME shot a wing off his *Wilma Elaine* and sent her plummeting to the ground, killing Smitty. They had been flying high, at some 3,000 feet; his passenger had a parachute and jumped out and survived.

My own experience at the Volturno River crossing is one that I shall never forget. We were standing there waiting for pontoons to be inflated when twenty-three planes appeared off to the northeast. An MP standing by my side said, "It's a good thing they're our planes."

"Ours, hell," I said. "They're MEs—look at those narrow fuselages." I dove for the bottom of a crater that had been made by one of our bombs when the Germans held this sector, and down the bombs came. I peered up over the edge and used the old English trick of pointing my finger at them; if the bomb seemed to rise above my finger, it would land behind me; if it dropped below my finger, it would land in front of me; but if it followed my fingertip all the way down, it would land on me, or very near, and this is exactly what one of them did. It hit about fifteen yards south of the river's edge, up on the bank in the crater, just fifteen feet from me. I was very dirty and very shaken up and was never so thankful in all my life for the bottom of a bomb crater.

Another Grasshopper encounter with the Messerschmitts occurred when Lt. Alfred W. "Dutch" Schultz was out on a reconnaissance mission. Seemingly out of nowhere an ME started after him. Lieutenant Schultz was frightened, but he tried to outmaneuver the plane. At this spot the terrain was relatively level. Suddenly in front of him he saw his chance to escape; he made a sharp left turn into a canyon running along one side of the sector. When Lieutenant Schultz returned to the airstrip, he landed, jumped out, and came running toward me, shouting, "Gimme a can of paint and a paint brush. I just got me a Messerschmitt!"

"What are you talking about?" I asked.

He yelled, "I got me an ME and I wanna paint a swastika on my plane!"

"Now, slow down," I returned. "Explain how you got a Messerschmitt with your little unarmed Piper Cub."

He told me that when the ME came chasing after him he dodged into the canyon. The German pilot thought he, too, could make the sharp turn into the canyon. But his plane lacked the ability to make the turn at the speed he was traveling, and he smashed into the canyon wall. There was an explosion, and the Messerschmitt plunged into the canyon floor below.[1]

It was November 14, 1943—it had been raining all day, so I hadn't done any flying and was just sitting in my tent. The flap blew open, and I looked out and beheld a sight of wonderment before me: the majesty of the lofty heights of huge mountains and the serene contentment of grazing sheep in the green valley below these great masters. Fluffy white clouds floated by, touching each peak as if to crown it with immortal glory, which they seemingly deserved. The long line of maple trees pointing the way to the white stone farmhouse in the valley shed their summer dress of delicately cut leaves recently tinted by Jack Frost and his merry helpers, making ready for the soft ermine coat that would soon be theirs. Now and then a tinkling bell could be heard in the distance, divulging the presence of lowing cattle munching the tender grass

1. This was such an unusual happening that it was later written up in the *Congressional Record*, H2100, no. 31–9, Feb. 17, 1944, H1871.

in the green pastures framed by a weathered rail fence. In the valley a small village was nestled, appearing to accept the protective care offered by the pine-clad mountain in whose bosom it so comfortably rested.

My reverie was broken by a volley from roaring cannons. Could this be part of the picture so serenely presented to me? Was this meant to be part of the Master's work I had just been viewing in awe? What could possibly be the connection between such beauty, splendor, and majestic scenes and the terrifying sounds of roaring cannons and the crackle of rapidly firing machines of war? Was it meant to be? Should children of the distant village be made to flee with their frantic mothers from such inspiring surroundings because the warlords were bent on destroying the power of others just to take it into their own hands?

Then the wind subsided, and the tent flap closed from my view the Master's work so beautifully done, and all was shut out but the distant roar of cannon and the drone of angels of death overhead. Someday the scene will come back and not be shut from view by the wind playing with the flap of my army tent, and it will live on forever as an exhibit of the Master as He would have it shown.

One time I was sent up on a mission to see if there were any towed guns going through a village off to the right of our sector. It had been reported by an observer that there were some. Lt. A. Cararie, my observer, and I took off and headed for that town. We cautiously approached the outskirts and could see a few small vehicles, which we at first thought were German reconnaissance cars. Later we recognized them as Jeeps. We flew closer in to the town and saw some trucks towing some guns. These were enemy guns, we thought, but we wanted to make sure, so we flew in closer, taking a chance at getting shot at. Lo and behold, they were the guns of the U.S. division to our right flank. All our nervousness approaching that town had been wasted. The next time a mission like that came up, we had them check the facts more closely.

Capt. Jack Maranelli commanded an air force typical of Grasshopper units. It never shot down an enemy fighter or dropped a bomb, but like the rest of us Grasshoppers, his little group was more detested by the German ground gunners than were the Flying Fortresses. Maranelli's command consisted of a cow pasture for a landing field, eighteen pilots, about the same number of mechanics, a few tents, and countless boxes of canned C-rations. Among his pilots were a dozen lieutenants and six sergeants. The sergeants had volunteered at a time when the pilots were selected from field artillerymen who had flown sixty hours solo and had pilot's licenses. Each plane carried a pilot, an observer, and a radio. Often there were not enough observers to go around, so the pilot had to do double duty. All pilots were skilled observers.

With no mess hall provisions, they lived for weeks without a hot meal. "We fly in crates and live out of tin cans," laughed Captain Maranelli. "The big news is that we haven't lost a single plane, and none of the men in this unit has been the recipient of the Purple Heart." Captain Maranelli himself had been chased by four Focke-Wulf 190s once but had given them the slip. "One 20 mm shell let a little fresh air into the cabin," he said, "but that was all."

We lived a rugged life behind the battle lines, moving with the guns, flying unarmed, and sleeping on the ground. We often landed downwind, especially when it was uphill. When we took off down the hill and downwind, it was like a roller-coaster ride back home. We studied the wind before taking off from tight spots and over high obstruction and sometimes squeezed over the tree-tops by flying very gentle S-turns. When changing positions, we often flew with our Cubs bulging at the seams, stuffed full of K-rations (lighter than C-rations), bedrolls, ropes, pup tents, and camouflage netting.

After landing near the front lines, we would quickly taxi our Cubs under sheltering trees or hedges. If necessary we would use our hatchets to cut bushes to cover our planes with branches. We would then place camouflage netting over the wings and tail. We put a dark cover over the windshields, staked down our planes, and bedded down our Grasshoppers for the night. Many times the enemy flew over our Cubs only to find that they had vanished into the landscape.

We Grasshopper pilots were happy to be doing what we did, not because of any glamour in our role but because we loved to fly. We enjoyed the challenges that faced us every minute we were in the air. We knew that good judgment, quick response, and accurate spotting of our targets would help end this ugly war sooner.

Lieutenant Lindsey, a fighter pilot, came down to our flight strip one day. He said, "Are you Lieutenant Cummings—Lt. *Bill* Cummings?"

"Yes sir, I am."

He said, "You know that we have a common friend, Gerald Lynn."

"Oh, yes, he was on a Mormon mission with me down in Argentina," I answered.

Gerald was a great guy. Everyone loved him. He had told Lieutenant Lindsey to look me up if he ever got in the same area with me. Before Lieutenant Lindsey left he said, "You know, Bill, I wouldn't trade you places for anything."

"What do you mean?" I asked.

A bunch of Grasshoppers. From left, Major Childress, Captain Clegg, Lieutenant Cummings, and Lieutenant Matlock.

He said, "Well, you're up there flying those little light fabric-covered planes right on the front lines. You get shot at, and I understand you get shot at morning, noon, and night. I have that P-39, and I have protection all around me, plus guns in my wings, and a nose cannon. Boy, I wouldn't trade you jobs for anything."

Several times we were shelled out of our own fields. I remember one evening when we had an exceptionally good supper prepared when all of a sudden, WHAM! Up went the center of our runway. We immediately sought cover in a nearby ravine. Hearing no more shots, we climbed out and went over to look at the crater. Lieutenant Board said, "Oh, that was just a dud that went off." About two seconds later—WHAM! again. When the shelling finally stopped, that good supper of ours was cold.

I had developed great faith in our secret weapons—that's what the Germans called our little airplanes, "secret weapons." In fact, they had even told their men that there was no use shooting at us because we, the secret weapons, were so armored that they couldn't shoot us down. It wasn't because they thought us so vulnerable, but because when they did shoot at us we could see them shooting and retaliate with heavy concentration of artillery fire.

All was not work; often we would visit Naples, flying over Mount Vesuvius and watching it belch hot lava. We flew over the Isle of Capri, Sorrento, and the ruins of Pompeii. And our food was not entirely C-rations; we managed to get greens, fruit, and wine from the Italians, who seemed more than glad to let us have them. I remember one time when I had to borrow an Italian farmer's harrow and drag a strip down the center of his wheat field before our Cubs could move up to this forward landing strip. I certainly could sympathize with the farmer. He wrung his hands in anguish but soon was soothed by one of the mechanics, who gave him a package of cigarettes. Later the farmer brought out wine and spaghetti to show that he had no hostile feelings toward us. We were, he said, their liberators.

Sometimes complications arose that needed immediate attention and possibly required changes in procedure to correct the situation. I remember this happened when there came through from Fifth Army headquarters an order that needed to be changed immediately. It was an order to set our radios on a specific channel that was constantly used by others.

I discovered that the radios in our aircraft would not function properly under this new setup. I went to the communications officer and said, "Major, would you mind putting out a memo to Fifth Army explaining that the radios in our liaison aircraft would not function properly under this setup?" I went on to explain, "In our headquarters' aircraft we could have a Fifth Army channel, and then the other channel would be our brigade channel. This way each one of the battalions would have the brigade channel so they could communicate with headquarters, the intermediate headquarters, and their battalion channel. They could then fire effectively and adjust. They would be in constant communication with their own unit."

The major turned to me and said, "Lieutenant Cummings, this is an order from Fifth Army, and you will comply."

I replied, "Can't you see the logic of it? Why can't you send a memo on through?"

He said, "This is the Fifth Army command. You *will* comply!" He then turned on his heel and took off.

I walked dejectedly down the path and saw Gen. Vincent Myer, who commanded the 18th Field Artillery Brigade. He asked me how things were going.

I told him, "I've been gradually getting your men in a position where they can create a liaison for certain needs in the combat area, rather than back in the training area at Fort Sill. They are coming along fine. But I received a disturbing order from the Fifth Army from our communications officer concerning this channel setup." I explained in detail what the order was and how it would be difficult for everyone when in the air—that we couldn't even use that channel because the Brazilians and all the Americans would be on it. Everyone would be on the same channel. I also explained that it would be impossible for us to use it in the air. Then I told him how it should be, just exactly how I had explained it to the communications officer.

He said, "How long would it take you to fly down to Fifth Army headquarters?"

I said, "Once I get down to the strip, it would take about fifteen to twenty minutes to fly down to Caserta."

"Okay, let's go," he said.

So we hopped into his jeep and went down to the airstrip. The mechanic cranked up the plane for us, and we took off. We landed down at the airstrip and went into artillery headquarters. As we walked in, a general I knew, who had been a colonel the last time I saw him, greeted us.

General Myer said, "Cummings here has a problem, and I would like you to listen to it." I told the general what the effect would be if our headquarters' plane had only two channels, the Fifth Army headquarters channel and our brigade channel. Then all of our battalion planes would have Fifth Army channel and their battalion channel. How would they communicate with headquarters?

He said, "It makes sense, and the order will be changed tonight and sent out to all units tomorrow." He then said, "Cummings, if you ever run into anything that you feel is essential for the furtherance of the work that you do, you have my permission to jump all channels and come directly to me." That *really* made me feel good.

General Myer and I flew back to headquarters. About a week later, I happened to see our communications officer. He came up to me and said, "What the hell is your idea of jumping channels? I told you that was the order and you were to stick to it."

I said, "Yes, but the order was wrong. It had to be corrected." I explained that I didn't jump channels, that I had told General Myer and that he had taken me directly to artillery headquarters of the Fifth Army. "After listening to the problem, they said it would be changed, just like I tried to get you to do," I said. "The general also told me that any time I had anything for the betterment of the Army aviation setup, I was at liberty to jump all channels and come directly to him."

The communications officer turned on his heels and took off. He never spoke to me after that. Sometimes when we have a little authority, we don't use it exactly right. We don't try to analyze the benefit. From experience, I've found that when any command comes down from above that you can see needs to be changed in order to bring a better result, you should try your best to get it changed, even if you have to jump channels.

One of the things I thoroughly enjoyed about being in Army aviation was that it was a new program. Even though we had been functioning for months, we still had pretty much free rein. Nobody yet had been able to come in and set up any rules that would be detrimental to its proper functioning.

One morning a Fifth Army L-4 landed on my airstrip. The occupants descended and headed up to headquarters. One of the passengers was a British officer. Later I found out he was Air Marshal Robert (later Sir Robert) Foster. When he returned to the airstrip to be flown back to Fifth Army headquarters, he looked in my direction, then came over and looked at the Grasshopper insignia on my leather jacket. He said, "Are you related to the Cummingses in Ireland?"

I answered, "I'm not sure, sir. I've been a damned Yankee since 1620. That's eleven generations back."

We shook hands, and he boarded the plane. That's the first time I had heard that Cummings was an Irish name, not Scots or English.

Another of the nice people to land at my airstrip and head up to headquarters was a fantastic hero in my book. Later he even became a greater hero: the indomitable Gen. Jimmy Doolittle, leader of the famous Doolittle Raid on Tokyo in 1942. When he returned to the airstrip to head back to Fifth Army headquarters, I walked over to him and said, "General Doolittle, would you honor me by signing my short snorter?" (I'm not sure how, when, or where the term "short snorter" originated, but during WWII it was often used to symbolize a bond of friendship among a group of servicemen. Sometimes a dollar bill was autographed by a visiting dignitary and by the man requesting the signature. Sometimes two servicemen signed one to signify a drinking pact between them; the bill was torn in two, and each kept his half for a future meeting, at which time he showed it. If one was unable to produce his, he would buy the drinks. But for my group of pilots and mechanics, the short snorter signified a fraternal pact of friendship.)

He took it out of my hands and said, "I will do so with pleasure."

As he finished, I pulled some new one-dollar bills from my pocket and said, "Sir, I have a bunch of good, yet bashful, men here who would also like your name on a dollar bill, so they can each have a short snorter too."

He grinned back at me and said, "Hand them to me. I'll be glad to." After he left, I distributed the dollar bills to my men, who were a grateful bunch of good mechanics.

Martha Raye and Bill in North Africa, next to his Piper Cub, Maggie the Faithful.

Many movie stars entertained the boys close to the front lines, but where we were, 90 percent of the time it wasn't safe for entertainers to come. I can truly say that the only female star I had the privilege of meeting was dear, sweet Martha Raye. She was uplifting to all of us Grasshoppers. That lady could sing like a bird and act like the best of the pros, and her jokes brought laughter and joy to us all. We were grateful to her and her troupe for coming into harm's way to entertain us and for spending time boosting the morale of us homesick GIs. These were great shows by very brave people.

In every theater of the war, the Grasshoppers were performing all kinds of assignments. During the invasion of Italy a couple of our pilots were on an "angels of mercy" flight. One of them was my good friend, Lt. Col. Paynee O. Lysne. His account in his article for *Army Aviation* illustrates the feelings we all had in fulfilling our missions:

We flew regularly to the new beachhead. However, this day we received an urgent call telling us they needed blood badly at the hospital. They said they had only 150 pounds of blood to pick up. When I got to the field I found 300 pounds, which was more than one Cub could possibly carry.

Another pilot volunteered to take 150 pounds, so there wouldn't be any of the badly needed plasma left behind.

When they flew out to sea there was such a strong, fierce headwind that they realized their gas supply would never hold out. They decided the only thing to do was take a shorter, more dangerous route, one that was closer to the shore. This route was in a German sector very heavily protected by antiaircraft. To keep from being spotted by the Jerries, they flew only eight to ten feet above the waves along the rugged coast.

Even though they flew within spitting distance of the German ack-ack batteries, the Germans held their fire. There must have been a guardian angel flying with them because of the life-saving blood they were transporting. The shortcut did the trick, and they arrived at their destination with maybe fifteen minutes of gas remaining. It was almost dark when they landed, and the blood was rushed immediately to the hospital. The hospital later called and told them, "So far, the blood you brought up has saved the lives of thirteen wounded soldiers. We just wanted to let you know how badly it was needed."

Lieutenant Colonel Lysne recalled, "I was still dead tired from making the trip, but that call gave me a lift. I would never do it again, though." Then he added, "Unless it was for the same reason."

· 8 ·

Return to Fort Sill

One day as I returned to headquarters, one of the GIs came up to me and said, "Lieutenant Cummings, are you going to do any night flying tonight?"

I said, "Sure."

He said, "That's great—we can get some sleep."

You see, we had found out something on our own and put it into practice. By doing a little night flying, we could achieve proper observation. It would stop the enemy interdiction fire, and the boys could get more sleep.

During night flying, after we had been out an hour or so, we would radio into headquarters that we were coming in. As we approached the field, they would hear us. There were seven empty C-ration cans, three on either side of the runway and one where we would come down and touch our wheels. They would put about half an inch of gas in the bottom of each can, and when they heard us coming they would light those cans. We had seven lights to guide us to the airstrip. As soon as we touched down, a foot went down over the top of each can, putting out the fire. This way the enemy could seldom find out where our airstrips were.

Ordinarily, each battalion had two aircraft and its own landing strip. They formed an independent unit within their own battalion. Then, of course, you would have the division headquarters, with its two aircraft, mechanics, etc. But sometimes, under certain conditions, it seemed it would be better if we could have a centralized field. Depending on the conditions, we would centralize the operations and would even have our own kitchens, where the men could have their chow, right down at the field. That was the purpose of the Centralized Field Program.

Under the centralized system, we had an operation board set up, and each pilot who came down, no matter which battalion he was in, would come into headquarters and give us (I was on a division board now instead of a battalion board) the latest information as to what he had seen up there and what was going on. In other words, this gave us immediate access to all the information from all of the pilots from the division.

Once in a while we found a maverick outfit out there that had been using its battalion field for so long it didn't know its headquarters division. It liked to run as a single entity with two aircraft for that battalion and forget the rest. However, we learned over a period of time when things should be centralized and when they should be turned back over to the individual battalions.

In October 1942, when I took over the command as flight officer of the 18th Field Artillery, the men were fresh from the States, pilots just out of school. They had their own ideas about our little world here in this battalion. When I brought up the idea of centralized control, they immediately voted it down because of the conditions at the Cassino front. That was before the invasion of Anzio.

I said, "Gentlemen, this is the way we have found it to work best under these conditions." They resented it, but within about three days every one of those men came up and apologized to me. They could now see the value of what I was trying to put across. I remember getting a letter from a Lieutenant Taylor, who took over my command when I was called back to Fort Sill. They had gone into southern France. He wrote, "Captain Cummings, we are still doing it your way; it is great, and the men really appreciate it." I felt very good for having done what I thought was the right thing at the right time.

We had one man who was a great guy, but he went forward on that single-field idea. Probably, he had been with an armored division and felt it was the best thing to do. It ended up that this man did finally see the point, and he became the one who was to write the new training manual for the department. I thought it was great, because when all heads come together, and everyone has an open mind, you can come to a beautiful, workable solution.

In December 1943 I was called back to Fort Sill to help indoctrinate the division on combat tactics and teach the new things we had learned. After landing in the United States and before going to Fort Sill, I had two important missions to fulfill. One was to visit my Uncle Dean at the Civil Aeronautics Administration in Washington, D.C., and the other was to go to Arlington, Virginia. On this day I was en route to Arlington, the home of Staff Sgt. James

"Smitty" Smith's family, the pilot who had been killed in that terrible crash during the invasion of Italy. As his former commanding officer, I was to deliver Smitty's belongings and his Purple Heart to his beloved wife, Wilma, and his daughter, Elaine, and his mother.

At exasperatingly frequent intervals the cabby would say things like, "How do you like being back home again?" or, "Did you see much action, lieutenant?" After a short answer, my thoughts would soon drift back to Smitty. It all was many months ago, yet everything that Smitty and I had done together seemed to be coming back to me. Each scene of the past year and a half was being reenacted as though I was going through it all over again.

I remembered the day that I stood by a pontoon bridge on the Volturno River and watched the Messerschmitts and Focke-Wulfs come over to drop their lethal loads and then turn back, strafing as they went. I didn't know then, as I jumped for a bomb crater to save my neck from the eggs of hell, that one of these German youths would at that moment be shooting Smitty out of the sky.

I recalled how fortunate Smitty had felt at getting away with a wrenched arm and scratched face as he scrambled out of his damaged *Wilma Elaine*. His number was not yet up. That Jerry didn't seem to have the bullet with Staff Sgt. James Smith's name on it. Nor did the two MEs that came out of nowhere just south of Cassino, shooting converging red streams of death in his direction. He outsmarted them that time, too.

Smitty always was a hot pilot. He made his little Cub do tricks that were unbelievable back in prewar days. His artillery pilot training was bringing excellent results. He had to be good. If not, the Luftwaffe would have extinguished him long before that unfortunate day in Italy. Like many other Grasshopper pilots, Smitty was often exposed to the deadliness of the ME-109 and FW-190, frontline antiaircraft, and small-arms fire. His family was very grateful to receive his belongings and the Purple Heart he had been awarded.

With this assignment completed, my next stop was Washington, D.C., to see Uncle Dean, who was then the research director of the Civil Aeronautics Administration. I had lost my license back in 1941 because I had passed out during the medical exam. In order to be able to fly after the war was over, I knew I had to get my pilot license back from the CAA, and I was here to do just that.

Uncle Dean introduced me to the new director, and I told him what had happened. After I had accumulated about 300 hours of flight time in the artillery, I had written to a Dr. Hermisheimer of the CAA, who had instigated the revocation of my license. I told him that I would like to have my license back, since I had now flown over 300 hours with all kinds of "brass" (up to three-star generals) in my little Piper Cub Army L-4 with no incidents. I said I wanted to be able to fly in civilian life when I got back home after the war. Dr. Hermisheimer's reply was, "Did you tell them when you put in for your Army flying that you passed out in Dr. Vance's office?"

Fortunately, I had gone in to see a Dr. Fraser, the flight surgeon, and told him the whole story. He said that it shouldn't have made any difference at all with this kind of flying, and he passed me. I sent that information back to Dr. Hermisheimer; he never answered my letter. Possibly he figured, "This guy will probably get knocked off, so I won't worry about him." I had my 201 file, which contained all of my military papers and records, with me, and the new director asked me to leave copies of all letters to Dr. Hermisheimer and all other records. He would see to it that I was back in the air as a civilian later on. With this errand completed, I was on my way to Fort Sill.

A short time later I received a letter from Dr. Hermisheimer saying, "We are glad to grant you a Class 2 medical certificate, inasmuch as you haven't passed out in all this time." Now I had my medical certificate commercial pilot rating. Finally, I was back in the air legally, both as a civilian and as an Army officer.

In a few days a packet of letters arrived from my uncle. He wrote, "Bill, I confronted Hermisheimer with the fact that eighteen Eastern Airlines pilots had passed out in the doctor's office, just as you had, and they were still flying, and that the pilot who took Roosevelt to the Casablanca Conference had passed out and he was still flying. Why can't my nephew fly? Hermisheimer had no alternative but to send you the letter that he did."

I had been assistant engineer officer in the Tactics and Gunnery Division at Fort Sill for about six months when the commanding officer of the division, a Major Watson, was called to go into one of the combat units. I took his place. In that position, I had the opportunity to use my wits to put something into play that would benefit the whole program.

In one of our activities in the Tactics and Gunnery Division, we would send pilots out to locate gunnery positions. We generally sent one or two gun sections out into the field, and at a predetermined time they would fire off several rounds of ammunition. The pilot would then try to locate those gun positions, which were camouflaged. They would see the flash of the gun and the smoke, pinpoint it on their maps, and bring the information back.

It came to me that we were sending a lot of guys out there to man those gun positions. That job could be done better and cost the government a lot less money and manpower if we recycled used shells. When I mentioned this to the head of the department, he said, "Now, Cummings, what are you talking about?"

I said, "Well, there are all those shells we throw away to be melted down into scrap, and there are powders that we take out of those shells that we fire into dilapidated areas to dispose of them. We can take some of the powder bags out and get a calculation on the new amount of powder needed, then put it in the shells, make a little stand for them, put a fuse in each shell, and send a couple of men out to light them. The light would come out of those shell howitzers and you'd still get the flash, the huff and puff, and the smoke. The boys could put several rounds of ammunition out that way."

He said, "I think that's a great idea. We'll try it."

Well, they nicknamed that little animal the "Cummings Howitzer." It was just another way of saving the government some money by using a little Yankee ingenuity. I found this to be true all the way through the whole Army setup, not just aviation.

Every GI had a good head. They were college graduates, they were bums from the street, they were men who had worked in the coal mines; they were men with good minds. They still had that good old Yankee ingenuity. Time and time again, GI Joe caused some of the best things to happen. I would often tell my men, "We have a certain problem here." Then I would tell them what the problem was and wait to see what solution they would come up with. Sometimes the lieutenants gave better solutions than the enlisted men, and sometimes the GIs gave better solutions than the officers.

After I returned to Fort Sill from the Italian front, and after being promoted to captain, I began working on some rocket gear that was new to the Army. I was sent up to the Naval Ordnance Station at Harvey Field, California, to check on the various tail services and other parts. I landed at the test services and went over to Operations to close out my flight plan. There I noticed a pilot sitting in the corner with a grin on his face and with his feet propped up on a desk.

He was a Navy lieutenant junior-grade combat pilot. He said to me, "Captain, do they pay you guys flight pay for flying those damn kites?" He looked familiar. I thought he may have been someone I had known at the University of Utah or in high school.

I looked down at him and said, "Lieutenant, do they pay you flight pay for flying those F4Us and TBMs and the rest of your aircraft that have all that armor plate under your butt, behind your back, and on either side of your body? Do they pay you flight pay with all those machine guns out your windows to fight back at anyone who shoots at you? Do they pay you flight pay with all that protection?"

"Hell, yes," he said.

"Well, lieutenant, I've got news for you." I continued, "Yes, they pay us flight pay for flying those damn kites, as you call them. We go sometimes two, three, four, five, even thirty miles behind the lines. They may be shooting at us with pistols, rifles, machine gun fire, and pompom artillery aircraft—you name it. We don't have armor plate under our butts, across our backs, and across our sides. We don't have guns to shoot back, excepting a .45 in our shoulder holsters. We have to dodge all that firing that comes at us. Yes, we get flight pay for flying those damn kites!"

He let out a roar of laughter, came over, put his hand out, and shook my hand. "Lt. Wayne Morris," he bellowed, with a smile. Now I knew where I had seen that guy—on the silver screen. He was a cowboy actor of sorts, and he had been called to active duty.

When my assignment was completed, I returned to Fort Sill and informed my superior officer that I had found the parts necessary to complete our rocket project. All our efforts were then directed toward finalizing and testing the effectiveness of this urgently needed new weapon.

·9·

Westward Ho

In March 1945 I was transferred from Fort Sill to the Naval Ordnance Testing Base in California, where I was assigned to head research and development for the U.S. Army Artillery Aviation Program. I was assigned a new airplane, a Stinson L-5, a larger and heavier plane than the L-4. The L-5 was twenty-four feet long and seven feet high. Unloaded, it weighed 1,477 pounds and carried 25 gallons of fuel. Its six-cylinder engine was rated at 185 hp, and it flew at 112 mph, slightly faster than the L-4. This was the plane I would be using for the upcoming rocket tests.

During March and April I was working on a rocket that was new to the Army. It had been an unsuccessful experiment for the Navy, which had passed it on to Field Artillery to see what we could do with it. In the Navy's experiments, a rocket with an explosive charge had been hung under the fuselage of a twin-engine drone. The Navy had had the drone take off from a carrier and aim into one of the Japanese ships, expecting to put that rocket right in the middle of some destroyer or battleship. The problem was that those drones were too slow, and the enemy would shoot them down before they could get within range. In the experiments we performed for the Army, the rocket was attached to the wing of my plane to see if it might be practical for an L-5 to fire it into caves housing Japanese gunnery nests.

While I was working on my rocket experiments, the commander said to me, "I have something here you could have used on that flight you made in the invasion of Sicily."

I asked, "What are you talking about?" He took me down to the strip and showed me a television camera mounted in the nose of the aircraft, and explained

Bill stands next to his new Stinson L-5, which he used for rocket and television experiments.

that I could have had a TV screen mounted in the back seat of my plane for the observer, aiming the camera at anything of interest. The image could be transmitted to the command post, which could then see everything that was going on.

The commander soon ordered us to put all our energy into the television project instead of the rocket experiments. By March 23 we had finished the installation of the television and an SCR 274N radio into my L-5, along with two transmitters and two receivers. The cockpit became quite crowded with all this extra equipment, but I overlooked the discomfort with eagerness to try the equipment out. With everything installed, the weight of the television was 245.5 pounds, making the gross weight of the airplane—with all gear, fuel, pilot, observer, and parachutes—a total of 2,364.5 pounds. The plane with full flaps maintained a speed of 65 mph. We made an actual test operational flight, with transmissions from plane to ground up to within a distance of about eight miles. The results were excellent. The observer on the ground received the best reception ever obtained in any such tests. We made shots of tactical targets such as moving ships (ground observers were able to distinguish on their screen the crew moving around on deck), an oil refinery, and a road network. All were clearly recognizable at the ground station. With the experiments successfully completed, we knew television would be used for all future invasions.

At this time the helicopter had also entered the picture, and Major Baker and I were to go to Chanute Field for initial training. However, other orders came from Gen. George C. Marshall, sending me to the Philippines to combat-test our rocket and television equipment. Capt. Bob Ely was assigned to take my place for helicopter training.

· 10 ·

On to the Philippines

The other branches of the service were by now aware of the Grasshoppers' success and began to demand light aircraft for themselves. The Cub had been used during the early stages of the war by commanders as courier and liaison planes. It now seemed that every major type of combat unit, except antiaircraft, found a use for the Cubs and borrowed them from the Field Artillery when it could fill some vital battle need.

The Cubs were highly commended for the superior work they performed on all battle fronts. They were particularly valuable in the Philippines because of the thick jungle, which they could fly over in a few hours. To travel any other way required cutting and chopping a path, a task that sometimes took weeks.

The Japanese were experts in the camouflage business, and some of their positions were truly masterpieces. We found this out early in the game, and from then on reports of a gun in a certain sector would bring a Cub in at treetop level to search all clearings until the gun nest was located.

One of our Grasshoppers, on an "angel of mercy" mission in the Philippine Islands, was flying to a rice paddy 900 feet long, the only piece of ground within fifty miles not covered by dense foliage and trees. His was a double mission: he was carrying supplies to a group of our troops who were fighting behind the Japanese lines, and on his return trip he was to evacuate a wounded soldier. The pilot approached the rice paddy and made his landing. As he left his plane, he realized no one was there. Suddenly, a voice called to him, "Start running, buddy! The Japs are 200 yards behind you!" Without waiting for further explanation, the pilot disappeared into the jungle. The Japanese were finally beaten back, and the Grasshopper pilot was able to complete his mission.

For the previous six months the pilot's outfit had been evacuating wounded, carrying supplies, doing observation, and performing other functions in support of the ground troops who were fighting deep in the jungle. It would have taken at least two weeks to slash their way through the jungle terrain to get medical help. The Cubs were able to make the trip in about two hours' time.

The normal duty of the Grasshoppers was to fly above the battlefield area looking for targets, like soaring eagles watching for their prey. However, on one particular day four of our pilots were flying a rescue mission for a group of infantrymen on patrol who had gotten into trouble in an isolated area just ahead of our lines. They were out of food.

Four L-4s, piloted by Lt. Bill Brisley, Lt. Charles "Speedy" Spendlove, Lt. Don Vineyard, and Lt. Raymond "Crash" Kerns, were each carrying on the backseats of their Cubs two cases of K-rations to be dropped to the patrol. They located the patrol on a narrow spur branching out from the side of a steep mountain ridge. There were deep vine-covered ravines on either side of them. The only way the rations could reach the patrol was if the L-4s dropped them and headed directly for the mountain ridge; the Cubs would have to pull sharply up to avoid crashing into the mountain. A missed target meant that the K-rations would fall into the ravine, where they could not be retrieved.

Lieutenant Brisley made the first drop, Lieutenant Spendlove the second, Lieutenant Vineyard the third, and Lieutenant Kerns the fourth. To prepare the package for drop, each pilot had to fly the plane with one hand while he reached into the backseat with the other, pulled the box forward down to the Cub's floor, and slid it up to the open door. Holding the box until he was on target, the pilot then pushed it out. The second run was to be performed precisely like the first.

The day before, Crash had flown into Japanese territory to fly out a prisoner who had been a member of Gen. Tomoyuki Yamashita's (commander of the Fourteenth Army Group) intelligence staff. To constantly be in eye contact with the prisoner, he had installed a control stick on the floor of the rear seat so the prisoner could sit in the front seat. The ration box fell against that stick and pushed it down. The Cub went into an immediate dive. He had only seconds, six at most, to release the pressure on the stick, or else. He swiftly loosened his seat belt, whirled around, grabbed the box with both hands and heaved it out the door. He grabbed the control stick and at the last moment pulled the plane out of the dive. With an enormous sigh of relief he joined the other pilots and headed back to the division artillery base at Loacan Field.

"That was a close one," he radioed to his partners after he regained his ability to speak. The K-rations had missed their mark by fifty yards and were lost in the ravine, but he had saved his own life...by a very few feet.

Every time a Grasshopper pilot went out to search for the enemy, help rescue wounded soldiers, drop rations to the stranded, or on any other mission, he faced death or a chance of never returning. I can't begin to tell of the countless times we faced the possibility of utter destruction. Yet our hearts and minds were set on our calling. We knew we were the only ones who were in a position to help in these situations, that the artillerymen depended on our achievements. So serve we did, each one in his own way, fearing death but knowing full well the outcome would nearly always depend on the proficiency of our Grasshopper Cubs.

Shortly after I arrived in the Philippines my brother Joe, who was serving in the Navy coastal artillery in the Pacific Theater, arranged for a six-day leave and made arrangements to spend some of the time with me. It was wonderful seeing him again. I arranged to fly him over the Philippines so he could get a good view of the islands from the air. He was awed by the splendor, color, and perspective of the aerial view. We often reminisce on that special time together so far from home.

There were four boys in our family, and we were all in different branches of the military. Mother and Dad had some anxious moments with four of their sons scattered over the globe during those war years. George was a paratrooper, Joe was in the Navy, Jack was in the infantry, and I was in Field Artillery Aviation. Our family had experienced the absence of each of us boys while we served two-year missions for the Mormon Church at different times. I had been sent to Argentina, Jack to Mexico, George to the Hawaiian Islands, and Joe to the northwestern United States. We four sons returned home safely. Each of us encountered much danger, but none received a Purple Heart.

A short time after Joe's visit, orders came through for me to report to Gen. Douglas MacArthur's Army headquarters in Manila. There I was told that I was to be the first pilot in the world to use television in air combat. During the last few days of the war, I flew with a television mounted in my Stinson L-5 into the jungles of the Philippines to test its feasibility. The camera was aimed where Japanese artillery was being fired, and the image showed up clearly on the television screen in my cockpit and on one viewed by ground control.

General MacArthur, after seeing what we could do with our "block gear," as it was known on these tests, decided that he wanted me to fly my plane and equipment during the invasion of Japan, doing exactly the job that my crew and I, with the help of the Navy, had designed it to do. I told the general that I had already trained his men in the handling of the equipment, but he said that he wanted me to fly it because I was better trained to do the job. The chance to take part in the military application of such a fabulous new invention as television gave me a feeling of excitement, but the thought of another invasion, especially of Japan, sent chills down my spine.

· 11 ·

End of the War

There we were, hovering over General Yamashita's "pocket" on the Luzon Peninsula, adjusting artillery fire on a nest of Japanese guns, using our artillery's newest gadget, television adjustment. Top secret at that time, it was referred to as the "block gear." I had been ordered by General MacArthur to take my experimental group and equipment to the Sixth Division to combat-test our television methods of artillery fire and equipment. This was much more advanced than the methods I had used on D-day in Sicily.

General McArthur said that if it proved as successful in that combat as it had been in a test we had run for him in Manila shortly before, we would use this technology in the upcoming invasion of Japan. Everyone had been dreading such an invasion, yet we felt it had to be. This was only a few days prior to the dropping of the atomic bomb on Hiroshima and Nagasaki.

I was not overjoyed when General MacArthur informed us that inasmuch as my crew had been working with the television equipment for six months, and since I had already been combat-trained in the Sicily invasion, he preferred that we handle the equipment on the invasion of Japan ourselves. He was reluctant to take the time to train a crew in one of the units already prepared to make the big push on the Japanese homeland. I had hoped that I had used up my share of invasions in Africa and Europe, but here was another D-day jaunt all lined up for me.

Then came that message over my radio: "Able, Baker, Charley Five."

"Able, Baker, Charley Three," I replied.

"Cease fire. End of mission. End of war. Return to field."

What beautiful words!

78

I responded with double emphasis, *"Roger, Wilco!"*

"Wilco" meant "will comply." Would I comply?! I looked back at Lieutenant Yonack and saw his broad grin and strong nod of approval as I made a tight left turn and headed back to the landing strip, as quick as the little L-5 could take us. Who wouldn't "wilco" on that one? You can see how welcome the words "Able, Baker, Charley Five" were for me. Those sweet words, possibly the last "end of mission" order given to a combat flight mission in WWII, became the swan song for the dreaded invasion of Japan.

The war was over!

And so I headed back to good old Fort Sill and the Department of Air Training. It was a twenty-day boat ride to the United States. (Just before we received our passage orders, I had sent a cablegram to my wife from Manila, telling her that I would be home very soon. This, of course, was before I knew about the slow boat.) Eventually, though, my train pulled into the Salt Lake City station, and I saw Maggie.

She said, "Bill, darling, where on earth have you been? I've been just frantic. I expected you home in a few days, and here it's almost a month!"

"Well, honey," I explained, "it happened that this colonel, who was sent overseas with us as nursemaid to help add brass to our party, decided that he wanted to get a Jap rifle home, along with some other trinkets. He decided to put them in one of the large empty boxes marked 'Top Secret Equipment' bound for Fort Sill, Oklahoma, and I was to guard it. Then we found that Air Transportation would not take heavy equipment back home without priority. Well, I'm just a captain, Honey, so it was a slow boat all the way home."

Many different branches of the service are given credit for winning the war.

How would we have ever gotten to the Philippines if the Marines hadn't taken all the islands in between?

No, the Navy won the war. How else could the Marines and the lowly infantrymen have reached their destination if the Navy hadn't transported them and neutralized shoreline installations, readying the islands for the occupation by the Marines and Army?

But who dropped the atom bomb? What about the thousands of blockbusters and millions of incendiary bombs dropped by the air forces, neutralizing enemy action so that ground forces could take over?

And the infantryman still thinks he's the one who won the war, not the flyboys, who went back to the soft life miles behind the lines playing poker and eating clean chow while the infantry ate mud with their K-rations and pushed the Jerries and Yamashita's boys back, inch by inch, until they both yelled "Uncle."

Now that *everybody* has won the war, I would like to say a little in the defense of a small group of men that were pushed around, discredited, and wrongly used until the combat troops began to see their value. Later moves wouldn't have been made unless this little group of men had been up front doing their job. I refer to the kite-flying Grasshopper pilots. I had the privilege of being one of the first in training and one of the first in combat. I observed the feats of these daring frontline kites flying from both theaters of operation, and I saw their value in all phases of operation, from the invasion of North Africa, Sicily, and Italy to the occupation of Japan.

· 12 ·

The Piper Cub

The Piper Cub had first been put into action by some of the Grasshopper pilots who were sent to England early in the war to act as coastal observers. They saw combat action later at Normandy. The rest of us and our Cubs were sent to North Africa, Sicily, Italy, and the Pacific. Piper Cub L-4s performed effectively in every theater of the war. We gave those Cubs a good workout. They were marvelous. Our Cubs did things that couldn't have been done any other way at that time. The Cubs cost only $2,200 each. (Just one of the Apache helicopters being used today in the military costs more than all the planes we had put together.)

The whole thing started with Army aviation. There is much history written about how the Civil Aeronautics Administration and all branches of the service worked with us. After a great deal of research and many exercises, the Piper Cub L-4 was chosen to be the eyes of the Field Artillery. In February 1942 an order was signed for 1,500 Cubs. In June 1942 the approval for organic air observation for the Field Artillery was sent to the commanding general of Army Ground Forces. From then on we got in the thick of it, and the combat action all started in Africa.

Many airplanes served great purposes in World War II; however, the Piper Cub clearly has a place in my heart. If someone were to ask me which aircraft I thought was the most important in that war, I naturally would select the Piper Cub. I would do so not because of any glamour or machismo associated with it but because of the outstanding service it performed during this difficult time.

The Piper Cub evacuated the wounded, transported generals, ferried supplies, and bombed and knocked out naval and artillery gunfire. This little aircraft operated out of very small fields, off beaches, and off roadways, most of the time right at the front line or just behind it.

Approximately 5,600 Cubs took part in World War II. The L-4 was feared by the enemy more than the deadly mosquito, with its threat of malaria. The enemy often sent squadrons to eradicate the Cub. But its speed of 65–75 mph and its maneuverability nearly always confused them.

Much has been written and filmed about fighters, bombers, and transports of World War II. But relatively little has been written about these Piper Cubs. The story of the Piper Cub in peace and war is the story of people who designed, built, flew, and maintained it. These Cubs were the ideal vehicles for the jobs they had during that period. But just as television has replaced the radio, and as the computer with its limitless capabilities has replaced the typewriter, the magnificent helicopter has gradually replaced the versatile Piper Cub. At the end of the war the U.S. government did not believe that the L-4 was worth the expense of reparation. Thus, hundreds of them were sold and used in the civilian sector.

My *Maggie the Faithful* made Grasshopper history. She was one of the first planes to take off and operate successfully during the invasion of Sicily. She was a veteran of the North African invasion and of the Tunisian, Sicilian, and Italian campaigns. During these actions my *Maggie the Faithful* flew some 760 hours, 485 missions. She was fired at many, many times but never received a bullet wound. (Unfortunately, sitting on the ground during one of the enemy shelling forays, she did receive a shrapnel tear in one of her wings.) During her course of service she received two new engines, seven new propellers, two sets of wings, a new tail, and new landing gear. Finally, she was put to rest to be used for parts. I do believe I wore my *Maggie* out.

· 13 ·

From the Piper Cub to the Helicopter

In the years 1940 and 1941 light-plane manufacturers and lobbyists contended that their small lightweight planes with speeds of less than 100 mph could help defend the United States. During maneuvers of the Second Army at Camp Forest, Tennessee, in July 1941, the Air Corps was asked to furnish some aircraft for observation. Piper and Aeronca each provided some lightweight planes with 65 hp engines, but these maneuvers were not considered successful, and the experiment was scrapped.

By mid-July the Third Army scheduled maneuvers at Fort Bliss, Texas. The orders were signed by Gen. Henry H. Arnold, chief of the Army Air Corps. The planes would report to Biggs Field for assignment to the First Cavalry. The pilots would be billeted by the Air Corps and allowed to eat in the officers' mess (this later was changed). The Texas maneuvers paid off. The aircraft performed their required mission, and they were durable and easily repaired. The Air Corps flyboys crunched their Consolidated Vultee O-1s so often that they were ordered not to land on any strip unless it had been used by the Cubs for forty-eight hours.

The Third Army went to Louisiana for the famous maneuvers held there in August 1941. Col. Dwight Eisenhower was in attendance; he had some flying time and flew one of the Cubs with a civilian pilot on board. During the fall maneuvers in 1941, Piper, Aeronca, and T-Craft furnished planes and pilots, mostly at no cost.

In December of the same year it was arranged to train Field Artillery pilots at Fort Sill, Oklahoma. Grasshopper pilots would have to be able to land anywhere and everywhere, if ever they saw combat. Their practice fields were primitive, carved out of the hills and trees. The purpose of this training was to turn out pilots for elevated observation posts. All the pilots had to be trained as artillerymen. They had to be able to adjust artillery as well as fly the plane. Liaison Pilot Class I started that July. After a training period that included sixty hours of flying time on fieldwork, road landings, artillery adjustment, selecting landings areas from the air, and a short course in airplane mechanics, the pilots were certified and shipped overseas.

The first Cubs were launched off the carrier *Ranger* for reconnaissance during the landings in the invasion of Africa. About this time the ground forces realized that several of the artillery battalions were short of planes and pilots. The Second Army Corps established a school in Sidi-Bel-Abbès, North Africa. The students came from various units. The school consisted of seventy-five flying hours, and on completion of the course, the eighteen pilots, with airplane, were shipped to those units short of pilots. The school disbanded after one class. My friend Lt. Col. Paynee O. Lysne, who was an Army engineer, was one of those who received his wings at that graduation.

Just prior to the invasion of Sicily, as I have described, an LST was modified with a seventy-five-yard-long runway built on the deck. Two Cubs were placed on it and were launched to reconnoiter and shoot the artillery. Other Cubs were brought in on trucks that had been transported in the LSTs. During the invasion of Italy at Salerno two more Cubs were launched off an LST. The Cubs were also used extensively in Italy and elsewhere in the European Theater.

In the Pacific Theater the Cubs were also used for reconnaissance and artillery observation. However, one of their main missions was medical evacuation. Some Stinson L-5s had litter compartments.

After World War II, general demobilization reduced the Cub inventory from around 3,000 to about 200, and Army aviation became a separate branch. In 1947 the Army acquired its first helicopters, the two-place Bell YR-13, and in 1948 a helicopter school was established at Gary Field, with training by the Army Air Forces (USAAF).

During the Korean War the Bell H-13 was used extensively as a "med-evac" vehicle by Army mobile hospitals. One Army aviator flew more than 950 med-evac missions, and all were successful. The Army also obtained the go-ahead for larger helicopters, such as the H-19 and the twin-rotor H-25. Then it moved up to a large twin-engine, twin-rotor CH-47, an excellent troop transport.

During the Vietnam conflict, the Army provided its own close air support with the Huey Cobra gunship and the standard Huey, modified with rocket pods and machine guns. The Army also had the twin-engine DeHaviland Caribou, which was used for resupply to forward units and as a troop carrier. Their motto was, "You call; we haul now." Today our active Army units are equipped with some of the most modern aircraft in the world, including the UH-60L Black Hawk, the CH-47 Chinook, and the AH-64 Apache, with more on the way.

Before the 1991 Gulf War broke out, I had an occasion to visit the large factory that produces the Apache helicopter here in my hometown of Mesa, Arizona. Joe Meyer and his up-line boss at McDonnell Douglas invited me on a private guided tour of the plant. After the close of shop for the day, we started from the beginning to the last Apache, ready for the final inspection and power tests. These babies could knock out a tank that could knock out a town.

· 14 ·

A Visit with Phil

Years after the end of the war, my brother Joe told me that someone at church wanted to see me, my longtime friend, Philo Farnsworth. I hadn't thought about Phil in years. The mention of his name brought to mind the circumstances of our first meeting.

It had been an extraordinarily beautiful day. I believe it was the magnetic pull of the day that led my feet to a lazily flowing stream up by the Boy Scout camp in the towering mountains of Utah. A warm sunny day, the majestic surrounding mountains, and a boy with fishing pole in hand—what a marvelous combination. The seclusion and tranquil moments while waiting for a nibble had a calming effect on me.

I noticed a few others fishing in the surrounding area, but there was one young man just downstream from me who seemed very personable. We decided to exchange some tales while waiting for a big catch. He told me his name was Philo Farnsworth and that he loved fishing but that his inventive mind had trouble keeping on the subject at hand.

Phil proceeded to tell me about his latest invention. I was particularly interested in this "television," as he called it. What an ingenious idea! Phil and I became good friends during those tender years, but after I graduated from high school I lost track of him.

A few days after Joe delivered his message, I went to visit Phil. He told me what had happened to his invention. He said a man that he trusted had come into his shop and stolen his invention of television for a very large company and that the Farnsworth family had been forced to sue that company. Phil and his family were having great difficulty proving that the invention belonged to him. In fact, he was close to losing the case.

Back in Idaho, a former teacher of Phil's found out about the trial. He was horrified. He promptly told his wife that he had to go to New York, where the trial was taking place. It happened that when Phil was sixteen years old, a few years before I met him, this teacher had assigned projects to the class members. When it came Phil's turn, he presented his invention of television. The teacher was highly impressed and told Phil to write the invention up in detail. Upon completion of the paper, his teacher helped Phil get it notarized and then filed it away.

Phil's former teacher found the paper and took it with him to New York. He walked down the aisle in the courtroom to Phil's attorney, presented the paper to him, and informed him that the notarized paper was the evidence that he needed in order to win the case. Astonished, the attorney presented the paper to the court and won. The large company was ordered to pay the Farnsworths $4 million before it could continue to manufacture televisions.

I informed Phil that I had mounted a television in the backseat of my L-5 and filmed battles in Corregidor and Manila and that the results had been so outstanding that Gen. Douglas MacArthur had ordered my outfit to use television in the upcoming invasion of Japan—which, thank God, never happened. He was extremely happy to know that his invention was being used in the defense of his country.

In 1971, not long after our visit, Phil passed away, possibly not aware of the critical role his invention would play in future wars. But before his death he had finally received the credit for his brilliant invention—the schoolboy dream that changed the world.

· 15 ·

Civilian Life

Back in civilian life in Utah, I continued in the Reserves. I was promoted to major on April 14, 1954, during my command of the Ninety-sixth Division of the Field Artillery Reserves. Being in the Reserves was nothing like combat; however, it did give me flying time, which I enjoyed greatly, and it gave me a continued relationship with some of the men I had served with during the war.

I ponder now on my experiences before the war and during my two-year mission in Argentina, where I taught the love of Christ without any malice toward anyone, and then in the armed services, where I was taught pure survival, even to kill or be killed. What a contradiction in action. My only consolation is that I never came face to face with those who reaped the fury of my artillery spotting. I didn't pull the trigger, but I did direct each shell to the spot of devastation. What will I be held accountable for?

War is on the opposite end of the pendulum from missionary work. As a missionary, I taught the Commandments and the importance of the obedience to them. I taught of a life hereafter, even eternal life with our families, through obedience to His Commandments. I taught honor and loyalty to one's country, knowing full well that in war my free agency in all these beliefs could be taken from me if the enemy should win. So it goes. One's heart must be, for a space of time, turned from those wonderful Christlike forces into a desire to survive, even through the horrors of taking another life or relinquishing one's own life in turn.

With some nostalgia, I have reflected on some of the experiences I have written about in this book. Being a Grasshopper pilot gave me the chance to fulfill the longing to fly that I had harbored from my youth. It afforded me the

Back in Salt Lake City after the war, Bill poses in front of the Utah Capitol Building.

chance to serve joyously my country during those difficult war years. I truly loved flying. Before takeoff I always had a moment of silent prayer, which helped keep that protective spirit with me. Sometimes in the thick of battle, like the invasion of Sicily, I sincerely acknowledged a divine protective power helping me through it. Had I not received my church's priesthood blessing before leaving for combat, I seriously doubt that I would have been brave enough to volunteer for that mission of no return.

I never hesitated to let anyone know that I was a Mormon. I remember that, due to the fact that I had served a mission for my church when I was nineteen years old, my pilot buddies nicknamed me "Mish." They would toss their full milk cartons my way, because I didn't drink coffee. And since I didn't drink alcoholic beverages, I was always designated to be the driver after a night out.

In civilian life I have continued serving in my church, working with Spanish-speaking members and teaching in various capacities. I served seven missions, the last with my present beloved wife, Kay, at the Family History Center in Mesa, Arizona. Long after I depart this mortal life, my missionary work will continue through the many ornamental iron animals, Wise Men, fountains, and other decorative lights that I made for the Christmas season at the Mormon Temple in Mesa.

As time continues, memories cloud and fade. I thank God for granting me the ability to express the experiences and feelings I had so many years ago during World War II. I loved serving my church as a missionary, and also I loved serving my country in World War II as a Grasshopper pilot.

Postscript

BY GWENDOLYN K. CUMMINGS

Bill and I met during the summer of 1982 in Mesa, Arizona, where he lived after his divorce from Maggie. We were married on February 17, 1983, in the Mesa Mormon Temple.

For years he struggled to write about his experiences during World War II, squeezing what little spare time he could from the obligations of his family and his thriving business. But over the years, advancing age and health problems began to take their toll. Finally, unable to maintain his demanding pace, he reluctantly gathered everything up, placed it in boxes, and stored it away. But his goal to tell the story of the Grasshopper pilots never dimmed. Bill hoped to someday complete the book, if God would grant him the time.

On July 4, 1999, as we sat in church, I glanced at Bill and noticed something was wrong. He had slumped in his seat and did not respond to my touch. A doctor was sitting nearby and quickly came to my aid. Bill was carried into the foyer, where the doctor examined him and then pronounced him dead. When he asked me if I wanted him to try to revive Bill, I had no hesitation. "Yes!"

He succeeded. Bill was rushed to the hospital, where his condition remained critical for several days. He spent more than a month convalescing in the heart unit. Coming back from his cardiac arrest was slow and difficult. His mind was still alert, but now his heart was too weak to allow him to return to his previous level of activity. He was confined to a wheelchair, with little hope of full recovery. It was obvious that Bill would not be with us much longer.

Knowing this, my family urged me to help Bill get his book completed before he passed on. They insisted that his life had been spared for a short time to give us time to finish the book.

Sorting through the four stored boxes, I found some writings, yellowed with age and crumbling to the touch. There were newspaper and magazine articles and pictures, many faded and some illegible. Some chapters were complete and ready to type, while others were in varying stages of development. With these materials at hand, my work began. There was much organizing to do. This was tedious, but Bill was too weak to do it. The process helped me gain a love for the subject. Sometimes he would read the manuscript, and often I would read it to him. At the end of each completed chapter, Bill gave his approval.

When the final chapter was down on paper, his frail body seemed no longer willing to continue. We had worked on the book together, cried together, and prayed together.

On February 17, 2002, Bill passed from this mortal life. It was a shock to the family, even though they had all watched him slowly dying over those few years. At his funeral his grandsons summed up his life with a most touching tribute to their beloved Papa. He had unconditional love for everyone. He was a great man, a great friend, a great and tireless missionary, a great storyteller. He judged no one. He was an inspiration to every family member, an outstanding example of patience, tolerance, and obedience to the Lord's Commandments. He wanted to bring the light of Christ to everyone. He made everyone he met feel like a lifelong friend. He was a freedom lover and had received high honors for his part in World War II. He is part of history, along with his ancestors, who had been among the early pioneer settlers of Utah.

Bill loved to talk. He especially loved to recount his experiences as a Grasshopper pilot. He was also a philosopher. One of his favorite sayings was "Live each day as if it was your last, but plant your garden as if you will live forever."